Assessing Competence

_in_

Higher
Education

The Staff and Educational Development Series
Series Editor: Sally Brown

Assessing Competence in Higher Education Edited by Anne Edwards and
  Peter Knight
Assessment for Learning in Higher Education Edited by Peter Knight
Research, Teaching and Learning in Higher Education Edited by Brenda Smith
  and Sally Brown

SEDA is the Staff and Educational Development Association. It supports
and encourages developments in teaching and learning in higher education through a variety of methods: publications, conferences, networking, journals, regional meetings and research – and through the
SEDA Fellowship Scheme. Further details may be obtained from:

The SEDA administrator
Gala House
3 Raglan Road
Edgbaston
Birmingham B5 7RA
Tel: 0121-440 5021
Fax: 0121-440 5022

Assessing Competence
in
Higher Education

EDITED BY
**ANNE EDWARDS
AND PETER KNIGHT**

KOGAN
PAGE

Published in association with the
Staff and Educational Development Association

First published in 1995

Kogan Page Limited
120 Pentonville Road
London N1 9JN

British Library Cataloguing in Publication Data

A CIP record for this book is available from the British Library.

ISBN 0 7494 1458 8

Typeset by DP Photosetting, Aylesbury, Bucks
Printed and bound in Great Britain by
Biddles Ltd, Guildford and King's Lynn.

Contents

Notes on Contributors

Alan Beattie is Head of the Department of Health Studies and Human Sciences at the University College of St Martin and Honorary Senior Research Fellow in the Department of Applied Social Science at Lancaster University. He has worked extensively in health promotion and community health in the NHS and the voluntary sector, and previously taught at the Institute of Education and at King's College in London. His contributions to the development of the theory and practice of health promotion have been widely published.

Chris Boys is Principal Adviser with the National Council for Vocational Qualifications. He has many links with higher education and he is currently helping to research the way that academics and others interpret the knowledge requirements of a sample of NVQ training and development units. He has been an Assistant Registrar with the Council for National Academic Awards' Development Services Unit and a Research Fellow at Brunel University.

Richard Carter is a Senior Lecturer in Engineering at Lancaster University and the Director of the Professional Development Unit of the School of Engineering Computing and Mathematical Sciences. He has special interests in engineering education and the development of professional competence.

Hugh Cutler, a geographer, is Director of Modular Combined Studies at the University College of St Martin. With his present appointment his interest in the development of transferable skills was further broadened in the context of a Combined Studies Degree programme. His current interest is in peer-assessment as a technique and as a means of measuring and encouraging student competences.

Anne Edwards has a personal chair in Educational Research at the University College of St Martin in Lancaster. She is currently researching mentor training in primary and secondary schools and the use of competences in the training of specialist teaching assistants. In addition to carrying out a range of other contract research activities through the Unit for Applied Research, she chairs the College Validation Committee and monitors the increasing use of competences in degree-level work.

Rob Halsall has a particular brief relating to external funding and external publications at the Didsbury School of Education, Manchester Metropolitan University. He has previously been Head of In-service Education and the University's CATs coordinator. His particular interests include 14–19 education, and teaching and learning in higher education.

John Hamilton was senior test development officer of the Cambridge-based Test Development and Research Unit before joining the University of Cambridge Local Examinations Syndicate. His work at the Syndicate has included the design of a 14–16 curriculum and a scheme of assessment (the International Certificate of Education). He is now Meno Project Director.

David Hustler, Reader in Education at Manchester Metropolitan University, has interests in teacher research, collaborative evaluation, learning environments and approaches to teaching and learning. Evaluation work includes the 'ROA and HE project' and the Employment Department's 'Guidance and Learner Autonomy' projects. He convenes an ESRC Research Seminar Group on 'Competences and Teacher Education'.

Peter Knight is a lecturer in Lancaster University's Department of Educational Research.

Bob Neal is a qualified engineer who has worked for the BBC in a number of fields, spanning engineering, personnel training and project management. He has worked as a director and as a consultant for the Alvey directorate of the Department of Trade and Industry. He is now manager of the Professional Development Unit of Lancaster University's School of Engineering, Computing and Mathematical Sciences.

Sue Otter is a Further and Higher Education Adviser to the Employment Department. Her particular expertise is in curriculum development models and the assessment of professional competence. She works closely with NCVQ and sits on the CVCP committee reviewing the development of vocational qualifications in higher education.

James Price is Head of the Department of Geography at the University College of St Martin. For the past eight years he has been working with other colleagues in the department on the development of transferable skills for undergraduate BA students. The move to a concern with competences and their development via, for example, peer-assessment, coincided with the introduction of the BA Geography course within the college in 1991–92.

Sam Saunders is currently Project administrator on the Leeds University Work-based Learning Project. He has been researching aspects of school-based teacher education, including a study of mentor thinking and a survey of competence profiles being used on secondary PGCE courses in England and Wales. His background is in teaching, with a particular interest in the integration of academic and pastoral aspects of the curriculum.

Peter Tomlinson is a senior lecturer in the University of Leeds School of Education. He was previously at the University of York and was before that a primary school teacher. His original training was in philosophy (Leuven), psychology and philosophy (Oxford) and educational psychology (Ontario Institute for Studies in Education). His recent work has been on the nature and enhancement of classroom teaching skill, which is the theme of his recent *Understanding Mentoring*.

Christoph Williams, Lecturer in Retail Management, has a first degree in Psychology and an MBA focused on Human Resources Management. He has worked both as an independent consultant and as an employee of a human resources consultancy. Since joining the University of Surrey he has conducted research into the management education needs of science graduates and has worked closely with a number of major retailers.

Richard Winter is Professor of Education at Anglia Polytechnic University. For many years his work has focused on professional education of a number of groups, including teachers, social workers, nurses and engineers. He has published widely on the methodology of action research, on the assessment of competence and on learning through the writing process.

Chapter 1

The Assessment of Competence in Higher Education

Anne Edwards and Peter Knight

CONTESTED CONCEPTS

This book is about competence and competences: a contested set of ideas in educational circles (Eraut, 1994). But more than that, it is about the insertion of the assessment of competences into the practices of higher education, which is itself a hotly contested concept (Barnett, 1992, 1994). Consequently we cannot discuss the assessment of competence in the university sector simply in terms of assessment and pay attention only to matters of, for example, reliability, validity and scaling. Any examination of developments in assessment in degree programmes has to be placed in the context of competing claims for the ownership and purposes of higher education itself.

The contributors to this text work in fields as disparate as education, engineering, geographical studies, health promotion and social work. Some operate in partnership with professionals, others see their work on competences as primarily student-centred and anticipatory of generic work-related performance skills. For a few of the contributors the major concern is the quality of the courses they give their students. Others take a broader view, examining the implications of competence-based assessment for the quality control of modular and franchised provision; for the emergence of a continuum of professional development which extends beyond the first degree; and for the complexity of the relationship between knowledge and skill. The chapters reflect a growing sophistication in the way that universities are tackling assessment issues, while also showing something of the range and scale of practices. These developments are evidence of the considerable adjustments made by the sector to meet the demands of increasingly powerful stakeholders in the enterprise that higher education has become. And here lies a tension we explore in this introductory chapter and find elaborated in contributions to the volume: in an exploration of the effects and implications of an emphasis on competence we cannot ignore the pulls of competing definitions of the purposes of higher education (Atkins *et al.*, 1993). But let us first turn to a rationale commonly provided for an increased emphasis on student competence in university sector provision. This rationale can be summarized as the need to change.

A CARICATURE OF TRADITIONAL ASSESSMENT

That schemes for the assessment of competence in higher education students are riddled with contradictions, problems and flaws there can be no doubt. The same is true of any attempt to make inferences about human capability, let alone inferences based on the deliberate, somewhat contrived sampling of a few performances. These difficulties are acknowledged in the following chapters and suggestions for their attenuation are made. But a consequence of this openness is that it might appear that competence-based assessment of learning in higher education is so problematic that the sensible person should stick with the known, tried and tested system that has prevailed since the late 1960s.

Yet familiarity is not the same as adequacy. We may know the more traditional approaches to assessment well and, perhaps as a consequence, overlook their distinctive features: the values that they embody, the imperfections that they perpetuate and the inequalities that they enshrine. So, before we consider some features of competence-based assessment, we shall review more traditional approaches to the assessment of learning in higher education. Many of these ideas are elaborated in a companion volume (Knight, 1995a, especially Chapters 1–6) and in Chapters 3, 4, 9 and 13 of Brown and Knight (1994).

- Propositional knowledge is more likely to be assessed than is procedural knowledge. Although there is plenty of evidence that employers value graduates who are able and disposed to *do* things (Harvey, 1994), what gets assessed in universities is learners' grasp of the subject matter.

- This propositional knowledge is often likely to be assessed through a narrow range of methods. The examination essay or the longer coursework essay frequently prevail. Not only do these methods limit the range of student achievements that can be sampled, they also encourage learners to concentrate on mastering essay writing, to the detriment of polishing other forms of communication. Yet, employers value graduates who can communicate well, both orally and in writing (*ibid*).

- It is difficult to mesh these assessment methods with the proclaimed aims of the curriculum. A course or programme may be designed to promote knowledge and understanding of a topic within a disciplinary area *and* be intended to develop, say, skill at working in groups and in oral communication. But sometimes the assessment system focuses upon the disciplinary goals and thereby marginalizes the other goals (in this case, groupwork and oral communication), with the result that students fail to take them seriously.

  Where what is assessed is less than what a course claims to be fostering, then assessment backwash will have the effect of equating the effective curriculum with what is assessed. It is for this reason that it is naive for quality auditors to look at course validation documents. The test of what a course actually offers is the course assessment arrangements.

- The assessment methods are opaque. It is seldom clear what is demanded by an assessment item (guides on essay-writing, for example, often just push the problem back a stage. A good essay may have an incisive introduction but what's that?) Moreover, it is seldom clear what criteria are to be used in assessing the work, let alone what weighting is to be applied to the various criteria and to their sub-components. Where criteria are specified they often beg more questions than they solve (so what are originality, analytical insight or critical stance?) Faced with opacity, learners are unclear about what they need to know, understand or do. It is hardly surprising, then, if they revert to ingrained strategies that owe much to what has been called a surface approach to learning, or regurgitation.

- Learners are easily disempowered by the traditional methods of assessment and can avoid taking responsibility for their own learning on the grounds that they have little control over what they are expected to do and how they are expected to do it. Yet, not only does this reaction obstruct attempts to encourage what have been called deep approaches to learning, it also runs counter to a common aim of higher education, that is the aim of developing autonomous, self-motivating learners. Moreover, the fact of being assessed, allied to the language of assessment, often makes learners feel hurt (Knight, 1995a, especially Chapters 2 and 4). These bad feelings may be detected many years later, even in successful learners.

- The methods depend entirely upon a community of discourse, upon the shared understanding of academics in a field, developed through years of experience of assessing and teaching. The system is not scientifically based, nor does it represent a gold standard. And there is a suspicion, fuelled by grade inflation, that where these standards change, they do so in response to structural pressures on higher education. Not surprisingly, there are some who wonder about the reliability (let alone the validity) of the system (Knight, 1991; Tarsh, 1990). 'It is hard to believe,' said *The Times*, 'that this steep rise [in the proportion of first class degrees awarded] is entirely the product of improvements in teaching or the nation's intellectual stock' (3 December 1994).

Traditional assessment methods also fit uncomfortably in a rapidly expanding higher education system. In the past five years universities have seen a massive increase in student numbers and a decrease in core funding. It is relatively easy to add more students to a lecture or seminar but the extra load on staff that comes from having to assess student work cannot be so easily accommodated. It appears the system that has operated for the past 25 years is in danger of collapsing in the face of the pressure of student numbers. Where it does not collapse, it might be prudent to ask whether coping strategies have been adopted that compromise the quality of the assessment process and hence the quality of the student learning experience.

We conclude that, at the very least, there are grounds for considering reform of the system for assessing learning in higher education. The assessment of competence represents a set of alternative approaches to the assessment of learning. While the pace is being set in England by the government-sponsored work of the National Council for Vocational Qualifications (NCVQ), particularly through its work on National Vocational Qualifications (NVQs) (Jessup, 1991; Boys, Chapter 2 in this volume) and General National Vocational Qualifications (GNVQs), other agencies are also at work. The range of activity represented in this book is summarized in Figure 1.1.

QUESTIONS ABOUT COMPETENCES AND HIGHER EDUCATION

There are various approaches to assessing competence in higher education, although the NCVQ's approach may be the most influential. As contributors to this book show, current work in higher education ranges from pragmatic activity in one course (Chapter 10), to more theoretically influenced work in another (Chapter 9), to widespread, pragmatic innovation (Chapter 3), and to systemic, principled initiatives (Chapters 2 and 4, for example). The shading in Figure 1.1 suggests a progression from the least powerful (lightly shaded) to the most powerful (more heavily shaded) forms of action.

	Pragmatic / tinkering	Theoretical/ principled	Both
Course or programme level			
System-wide[1]			
Both			

1. System-wide could refer to a national inititive, such as GNVQ development at higher levels, or to a university-wide initiative (for example that at Oxford Brookes University, described in Chapter 3).

Figure 1.1   *A range of competence initiatives*

The insertion of competences into the curriculum and assessment framework operated by universities is clearly an innovation that is being grasped and adapted by some in higher education. However, whatever the purposes or shape of innovation, questions ought to be asked about its quality. Quite properly in this collection we wish to consider the following perspectives on competence:

● The philosophical bases of the assessment of competence. For example, what ontologies and epistemologies underpin an approach to the assessment – and hence to the specification – of competence? What assumptions are being made about the nature of human experience and of human capability? Is it reasonable, for example, to distinguish procedural knowledge from propositional knowledge, or to assess the one (propositional knowledge) through displays of the other, or to value one more highly than the other?

● The psychological bases of the assessment of competence. May competence be characterized in terms of general, transferable skills, or are contextual factors critical to *any* performance? May we speak in terms of levels of competence, of hierarchies? What distinct competences or clusters of competences can we identify? How do we handle a fundamental assessment problem that any given performance does not necessarily represent a person's competence? What about the technical but important issues of validity and reliability?

● The sociological ramifications of the assessment of competence.

What social purposes are competences serving? What is the impact of an emphasis on competence on higher education? What is the impact on the professions and their relationships with the university sector? How does this mode of assessment affect relationships between students and tutors, and between students, tutors and mentors? Is one social group more advantaged than another by this form of assessment?

- The practical issues. A clean bill of health on philosophical, psychological or sociological grounds does not mean that the system is workable, and we have the recent example of the assessment of learning in the English National Curriculum for schools to act as a reminder that good intentions may not be realizable in practice.

  There have been fears that the assessment of competence through NVQs can be very expensive to do properly, so before proceeding with the assessment of competence in higher education, we would need to be reassured that it would not prove to be costly, paying particular attention to the demands it would make on academic staff time.

  There are also substantial staff development implications. Not only is there the issue of providing sufficient, high quality staff development, there is the more fundamental issue of how far staff development *can* change academics' attitudes and practices.

  Third, there are issues to do with university organization. British universities are not, in the main, geared up to manage university-wide change (see, for example, Brown and Knight, 1994, part 4; Knight, 1994). Yet, that is exactly what is implied by a model of core competences, for it would be patently unfair for a university to encourage only some of its learners to develop competences that are in demand by employers, given the view that these are competences that can be developed in any disciplinary context.

  Fourth, it is one thing to define competences and to have views about their assessment but it is quite another to have a pedagogy for competence. How learners are to be ushered towards competence remains problematic, all the more so now that problems are being seen with the catch-all solution of fostering 'reflection' (see, for example, Eraut, 1994). The issue of pedagogies for competence needs a book of its own.

Clearly the incorporation of competence-based assessment in the practices of higher education challenges commonly-espoused values and routines of assessment. The question remains of whether the challenge should be welcomed. With this in mind, we turn to an overview of the NCVQ experience of the assessment of competences.

SEEKING A BALANCE: THE NCVQ APPROACH?

It is helpful to rehearse some of the positive claims that have been made for the assessment of competence, especially in the form advanced by the NCVQ (see also Chapter 2 in this volume):

- It encourages a broad curriculum by directing attention to the promotion of a wider range of attainments than those encouraged by traditional assessment systems.

- This wider range of attainments meshes with the qualities that employers value in graduates and which the government wishes to foster.

- It may be claimed that these qualities are not at odds with traditional liberal education and, indeed, that they are implicit in the notion of the educated person.

- It can sharpen both teaching and learning by making it clear to all participants, including workplace mentors, what has to be demonstrated if competence is to be accredited.

- It can enhance motivation through providing a set of clear targets that learners can tackle at their own pace.

- It favours flexible curriculum structures and pedagogies, since it is only the learning outcomes that are specified, not the means by which they are achieved. Universities and individuals are free to work towards mastery of those goals using whichever methods they find appropriate.

- It provides a structure for the accreditation of prior learning (where candidates will be able to present evidence of prior achievement in terms of competences) and of prior experience, where it will be open to applicants to show the learning that has come from their experience by providing evidence of it so as to demonstrate competence according to GNVQ, SVQ or NVQ requirements.

- Learning and assessment will often be in real-life settings, which should be beneficial to the learner and enhance the authenticity of the award.

- The NCVQ assessment frameworks of competences, elements and range statements are based upon systematic analysis, research and critical reflection and represent the state of the art at the moment.

- The NCVQ awards are national, marketable and transferable.

- NCVQ-sponsored assessment is based upon arrangements to ensure that there is reliability and validity on a national scale.

- The perceived imbalance between procedural and propositional knowledge may be redressed in the variety of the evidence required (Mitchell and Bartram, 1994).

- The assessment whenever possible of propositional knowledge through performance (procedural knowledge) is a parsimonious approach to assessment.

- The system is well-suited to profiling and to Records of Achievement, hence to formative assessment, learning contracts and negotiation.

None the less, many issues remain. Of particular interest is the future of the assessment of competence in non-vocational programmes. While this book includes an example of the assessment of competence in a non-vocational course (Chapter 10), most activity on the assessment of competence has taken place on vocational courses, as contributions to this book show. But is this a necessary feature of the use of competences in higher education provision, or is it a feature of *this* stage of work in *this* country?

Here the theme of Chapter 12 is relevant. Williams argues that GNVQs, which are not as tightly linked to specific occupations as are NVQs, are gaining ground in the pre-university sector and that they will exert an influence on practices in teaching, learning and assessment in higher education in general. Alongside that we set the development of GNVQs to embrace levels 4 and 5, that is levels which would be appropriate to higher education courses. Some of the competence statements will relate to general, or cross-curricular, skills and be as applicable to an engineering programme as to a French degree or to a BSc in astronomy. An important consequence of any such development would be that the assessment of competence would change from being an interest of those concerned with professional learning to being a pressing concern for those who are concerned with higher education, irrespective of the subject or area of study.

Currently there is no public move to extend the National Curriculum by developing a core curriculum for our mass higher education system. Yet, this could be an attractive proposition to some politicians. Not only would a core curriculum based on competences allow claims to be made that higher education is contributing to the stock of human capital that the nation requires, but it would also permit league tables to be constructed, performance indicators to be used, accountability to be exercised, consumer choices to be rationally made and appraisal of academics to be rigorously conducted. GNVQs or some other definition of competence in the so-called general, transferable skills could constitute this core. The assessment of these competences could come to drive British higher education in much the same way as testing programmes drive some North American colleges and universities. This is not to say, of course, that a sympathetic stance to the assessment of competence must lead to a national core curriculum for higher education. It is to recognize that a nationally-agreed framework of competences and their assessment carries with it possibilities that state control of higher education may be extended, much as it has been in the school system.

If universities do not quickly pool their expertise to put in place assessment systems that reassure government that worthwhile learning is taking place and that standards are being maintained and enhanced, then there must be a chance that government will take a handy tool, such as the NCVQ approach to the assessment of competence, and use it for purposes of accountability for which it was never designed.

COMPETENCES AND THE CONTROL OF HIGHER EDUCATION

Relevance is currently a powerful theme in discussions of higher education. Its importance is reflected in institutional mission statements and in the ubiquity of 'fitness for purpose' as a technique for aligning course design and assessment to institutional mission and with relevance to the concerns of the 'stakeholders' in higher education. The emphasis on relevance privileges those stakeholders who are users of the products of higher education as relevance is frequently measured in terms of current national economic needs. This definition of relevance in course provision in higher education also appears to be in tune with other performance indicators in, for example, university research ratings which similarly emphasize relevance to users.

There have been fears, therefore, that the current drive to assess competence, so easily tied to user definitions of relevance, represents an extension of government or social control over higher education. Taking a Foucaudian position, we could argue that the assessment of competence, as currently conceived by government, represents a substantial increase in surveillance of higher education and is set to become the panopticon from which all university learning is surveyed. The extent of surveillance is increased through assessing personal qualities and competences that have hitherto been seen to lie outside the remit of higher education. So, not only does the state become placed to survey the whole system but it is also empowered to survey the 'whole person'. This might also be understood from a Habermasian perspective. On this analysis, modern capitalist states have an interest in diverting attention from moral issues to do with ends, goals and purposes, redirecting it towards questions of techniques, means and methods for advancing the purposes *which the state specifies.* Given the origins of the NCVQ, created by government to promote *vocational* ends, it is possible to understand the current debate over the assessment of competence as essentially a technical debate that distracts attention from the larger question of the purposes of higher education which have recently been stimulatingly discussed by Barnett (1994).

The recent and rapid expansion of higher education in an era of consumer choice and managerialism has produced a perhaps less insidious university-based control function for the use of competences. The higher education machinery of validation and quality control is finding that it needs to attend to the unwieldy nature of modularization, franchising, and workplace training. Assessment of competence can appear a convenient way of gauging student experience (see Chapter 3). But entirely appropriate concerns with quality control may have wider repercussions. Managerialist concerns with accountability may accelerate a dramatic refocusing of higher education away from what has been its traditional curriculum and scholarly concerns.

These repercussions are evident in the extent to which competence remains a contested concept in higher education. Competences may be seen in entirely operational terms and directly related to specific practices. Alternatively, they may allow a more psychological interpretation which, using neo-Vygotskian frameworks, allows an emphasis on mastery of a curriculum and its discourse. Such a psychological, neo-Vygotskian interpretation would recognize the importance of the end-point assessment of skills and understanding but would see that as simply the tip of the pedagogic iceberg and would emphasize the curriculum and ways in which students might learn. The tension lies in a distinction between an emphasis on the assessment of key aspects of performance in context and an emphasis on the developing knowledge culture of the subject or profession into which the student is being inducted. By stressing the performance, higher education may be attending to cost-effective quality control but may be paying insufficient attention to the quality of what the university sector might contribute to society in, for example, the development of knowledge. Beyond issues of course design, operational definitions may mesh also with aspects of research funding to reduce the role of higher education as a source of fresh ways of seeing.

The need for cost-effectiveness and the existence of a new managerialism in parts of higher education may combine to warrant a performance-based competence culture which arguably tends to diminish the scholarly bases of traditional universities. It could be claimed that this culture of competence colludes with attempts to create a tiered system of higher education in which different grade institutions offer different experiences and create different 'products'. To return to earlier discussions in this chapter, much will depend upon the rationales adopted by institutions for their use of competence-based assessment and on the definitions of competence developed through those rationales. At the centre of any rationale would have to be the nature of the 'product' of the degree programme.

COMPETENCES AND THE CONTROL OF THE LEARNER

Competences are frequently presented as student-centred and can be important elements in learning contracts: Chapter 6 gives an example from teacher training. Clarification of performance goals as part of a learning contract between tutor and student is also fundamental to what is often termed flexible learning in higher education. Yet much depends on the purpose of flexible learning schemes.

If schemes are established to enable tutors to manage large groups, then agreed learning goals ensure that learners remain on target with minimal supervision. They become the self-monitoring semi-agentic beings who, although not responsible for goal setting – this is arranged at validation – are at least in control of movement towards that goal. They become the self-monitoring beings vital to the survival of democracy described, for example, by Rose (1990). Self-assessment, so frequently a feature of this model, simply enhances students' understandings of how the goals are interpreted in the culture of the subject of study and aids the students' self-monitoring. Evidence on the use of self- and peer-assessment (see Chapter 10) suggests that students get better at it with practice and that investment of tutor time in training for self-assessment may have long-term benefits in the form of a reduction in student dependency as learners move towards agreed curriculum goals.

If, on the other hand, the aim is to enhance student capacities for learning and a reference to metacognition is invoked (see Chapters 3 and 11), a stronger argument may be made for the quality of student experience. Yet it may be necessary to ask whether competences are essential elements in this experience. Focus on competence can more-over lead to a 'desert-islanding' of the student (or of the student and the tutor or the mentor) and can preclude attention to the contexts in which competence is acquired and developed (Edwards and Collison, in press). Its quality control implications are clear as the focus allows for individual blame rather than corporate responsibility.

From a learning perspective, such a focus on individual performance datedly ignores the importance of knowledge cultures, situated knowledge, the varied opportunities provided by the learning situations encountered by individuals and, particularly, the value of teaching as a language-led induction into the conventions of an area of study. Individual performance, though important, is arguably only part of what should be assessed.

Attention to competences closely linked to relevance to the needs of the immediate users of the products of higher education advantages graduates who enter the job market. But again performance-based competence may not be the only way forward (see Chapter 7). Training students to be able to analyse their own rich experiences in order to identify competences relevant to specific fields may be ultimately more conducive to creating the autonomous, self-motivating learner required by higher education, industry and business alike.

COMPETENCES AND THE CONTROL OF THE PROFESSIONS

Competences in higher education, in the majority of instances, make their appearance in degrees that focus on preparation for specific (para) professional groupings and most frequently in those that demand an element of workplace training. The most obvious examples are teaching and the health-related professions. This is certainly the case in this volume. In these contexts competences need to be examined in relation to the training partnerships that exist between higher education and these professions.

The nature of these partnerships is, despite common memoranda of cooperation, rarely homogeneous, even within a profession. This variability indicates the extent to which the particular roles of each training partner are being continuously redefined both in relation to their own workplaces or organizations (Edwards, 1994) and in relation to competing views of how and where professional knowledge may be best acquired.

But partnerships relating to professional preparation in reality rarely comprise only the two training bases. Professional bodies and, in the case of teaching, the Department for Education (DfE) have a role as influential, if sleeping, partners. Responses to a series of questions about the origins and assessment of competence give some measure of the nature of the partnerships that obtain between higher education, professionals and their professional bodies:

- Who devises and approves the competence statements?

- Who makes the formative assessments?

- Who makes the summative assessments?

- Who confirms the award?

- Who creates the assessment guidelines?

Answers to these questions inform us about the following issues:

- The relative strengths of different (para)professions as professions.

- The extent to which competences are being used by the professional bodies (or the DfE in the case of teaching) to control professional performance.

- The extent to which an emphasis on 'performance' may limit the knowledge base and understanding of professionals.

Chapter 5 suggests that with sufficient attention to the rationale for competences and recognition of the potential complexity of the assessment process, higher education can work with professionals to ensure that deprofessionalization is not an outcome.

Without an engagement with the complexities of professional knowledge in action, higher education's workplace-based partners may find that they are being called upon to collude professionally in the erosion of a professional knowledge base, however ineffable that base might be to practitioners.

These are interesting times for some professions. Managerialism is evident not only in elements of higher education but also in, for example, the health service. It can be argued that a competence-based simplification of the work of the professional groups we have been discussing coincides with an erosion of their professional tribal boundaries in the name of, for example, inter-professional care. Postmodernism and the Conservative party may be said to walk hand-in-hand in a managerialist world. Let us, therefore, return to our earlier reference to competing views of where professional knowledge may be best acquired. If one possible outcome of competence-based assessment is the erosion of professions, it may be that the energies of workplace and higher education partners would be more fruitfully directed at sustaining the professionality of these professional groups. Higher education should perhaps collaborate more extensively with the professions to that end through a research-based elaboration of the origins and purposes of the components of professional action and of ways in which this competence might be validly assessed.

Moving beyond those professional partnerships to look at higher education teaching and research as a profession in its own right, one can see similar processes at work in the use of competence as a cohering mechanism in modular degrees. As the cultural knowledge bases of subjects receive attacks that parallel those on the specific cultures of professions, control of the supra-disciplinary competences associated with, for example, definitions of metacognition as sets of learning strategies, become important to higher education managers and those who monitor them through national quality control systems. Depth of subject study may be lost, and tribal subject boundaries eroded. At the same time, universities can warrant their existence in terms of 'relevance', despite the loss of the power of their traditional discipline bases, and interestingly of the professional scholars who develop them.

INCORPORATING COMPETENCES INTO DEGREE PROFILES

The big question remains. What is the impact of the assessment of competence on the award and classification of a degree? Transcripts of academic performance on modular units may be supplemented by information on associated competences. Graduates may increasingly carry with them records of achievement which become the starting point for their further professional development (see Chapter 7). But the fate of pupil records of achievement in the employment market does not encourage acceptance of these records as *the* solution (Knight, 1995b).

One answer seems to lie in increased collaboration between higher education and professional groups. Chapter 4 gives one example of the extent to which this is important in social work training. But the example from the field of engineering in Chapter 9 shows how higher education may take the lead in a carefully researched analysis of how competences may contribute to, in this case, the award of a Master's degree. However, it may be that the knowledge and professional culture of some professions, such as engineers, are more amenable to this approach than is the case with, say, health visitors.

Higher education does not have simple responses to the complex issues that have been rehearsed in this introductory chapter. Yet we are convinced that the research and subject expertise to be found in the university sector is combining with a willingness to engage with important professional issues and a commitment to student learning to ensure that these issues are being tackled and redefined in creative ways.

Our analysis would suggest that the challenge is to weave together:

- relevance (and best bet ideas about future relevance) to industry and business;

- the cultural bases of subject knowledge;

- the cultural bases of professional knowledge;

- assessments that capture with validity the relevance of the student experience to the professional and/or subject-based aims of courses;

- assessments that are sufficiently reliable to dispel the fears of quality monitors;

- programmes of study that mark competent performance as a desired outcome but which attend to the learning needs of students as they move towards competence.

We think that the contributors to this volume have taken important steps to meet this challenge in relation to assessment.

Chapter 2

National Vocational Qualifications: The Outcomes-plus Model of Assessment

Chris Boys

INTRODUCTION

There is more to the National Vocational Qualification (NVQ) model than behavioural 'outcomes', although they remain central to it. The model is continually evolving and improvements are being made to ensure that the National Council for Vocational Qualifications (NCVQ) meets the aims set for it. These aims were first given in a review of vocational qualifications undertaken by a group chaired by Oscar De Ville (MSC and DES, 1986). NCVQ's model must be evaluated in terms of the intentions set for it, although many in higher education may not be familiar with them.

The review recognized both strengths and weaknesses in existing vocational qualifications. The weaknesses included: no clear, readily understandable pattern of provision; considerable overlap and duplication; gaps in provision; many barriers to access to qualifications and inadequate arrangements for progression and credit transfer; assessment methods that were biased towards the testing of knowledge rather than skill or competence; insufficient recognition of learning gained outside formal education and training; and no effective national system for vocational qualifications. The review recommended the establishment of a National Council for Vocational Qualifications with a remit to reform the system of vocational qualifications through the creation of a national framework to provide:

> a classification and hallmarking system for vocational qualifications that will secure standards against national criteria and simplify routes of progression to the higher levels of achievement (MSC and DES, 1986, p. 19).

Vocational education is a major part of higher education and it is important that academics understand the nature of NVQs, levels 3–5 of which are summarized below. Higher education will be interested mainly in the higher levels of the model, the number of which is growing and expected to increase over the next few years, although they still only account for a minority of all NVQs. There are currently 90 NVQs at level 4, representing 13 per cent of the total number of NVQs, and there is only one NVQ at level 5.

Level 5: competence which involves the application of a significant range of fundamental principles and complex techniques across a wide and often unpredictable variety of contexts. Very substantial personal autonomy and often significant responsibility for the work of others and for the allocation of resource feature strongly, as do personal accountabilities for analysis and diagnosis, design, planning, execution and evaluation.

Level 4: competence in a broad range of complex, technical or professional work activities performed in a wide variety of contexts and with a substantial degree of personal responsibility and autonomy. Responsibility for the work of others and the allocation of resources.

Level 3: competence in a broad range of varied work activities performed in a variety of contexts, most of which are complex and non-routine. There is considerable responsibility and autonomy, and control or guidance of others is often required.

Some universities and other higher education institutions are centres for assessing NVQs, either as part of academic programmes or for their own staff. The Open University is an awarding body for some NVQs as is the Management Verification Consortium which acts as an umbrella organization for a number of universities offering NVQs in management or training and development. The Open University is undertaking a project which, among other things, aims to produce specific Pathways Guides to encourage and enable students to prepare successfully for NVQ assessment as well as – or instead of – conventional academic assessment. The Employment Department has funded projects on the integration of NVQs in higher education and on credit accumulation and transfer involving NVQs. There is a possibility that higher level GNVQs, at least at level 4 of the NVQ framework, might be introduced in the future.

There are several characteristics of NVQs that I want the reader to bear in mind and see as possible correctives to some of the common misunderstandings about them that seem to be widespread in higher education:

- Although they have to conform to NCVQ criteria and adopt a common format for specifying outcomes, NVQs are not monolithic, inflexible structures and vary, for example, in their core and option structures.

- Where valid in the assessment of competence, formal tests of knowledge may be used in NVQs to support other evidence. Indeed, methods of assessment are diverse although they all have to be work-based. They may include simulations where it is not feasible to collect evidence from an actual event.

- NVQs have been criticized for not assessing knowledge and understanding sufficiently. NCVQ takes this criticism seriously because it has always maintained that principles and theories necessary for performing to the standards set for an occupation must be specified and assessed. To what extent this can be assessed through performance, portfolios, or through separate tests or examinations is determined by the nature of the competence and the range of contexts to be covered.

- NVQs are about professional expertise. Seen in this light, the reservations that higher education may have about NVQs may be no different from the general reservations it may have about teaching and assessing in professional spheres.

My final introductory remarks are the usual sort of riders: the views expressed here are mine and do not necessarily represent the views of my colleagues at NCVQ or official policy. Any errors of fact or judgement are, of course, also mine. What I have to say should be considered as an attempt to share some impressions and thoughts about some difficult subjects and not as an indication of NCVQ policy.

SPECIFYING OUTCOMES

The De Ville Review (MSC and DES, 1986) said that a vocational qualification, defined as a statement of competence clearly relevant to work, should incorporate the assessment of skills to specified standards, relevant knowledge and understanding, and the ability to use skills and to apply knowledge and understanding to the performance of relevant tasks. Stress was laid on making the qualifications more informative, especially in indicating the competence of an individual. The NCVQ, together with the Employment Department, devised a method and a format for specifying competence to meet the De Ville remit. It is important to realize that the specification of competence is a national specification of what is to be *assessed* and not a specification of a *learning programme*, thus, and as required by the De Ville Review, allowing for the assessment of outcomes whether these are learned as part of a formal programme or not.

Specifying clearly what a candidate has to do in order to be judged competent to perform to the high standards required under real working conditions has the following advantages:

- it provides an index for identifying whether qualifications or units are identical, thereby helping to create a rationalized national system of qualifications with greater opportunities for credit transfer and mobility within and between occupations;

- assessment is tied to the performance of what is required in an occupation and guarantees that someone who successfully meets those standards can perform in real work settings;

- learners can know in advance what evidence they need to collect and can negotiate with employers, potential providers of programmes and assessors about the means for collecting that evidence and determining whether they have achieved the level of competence stated;

- learners can retrospectively evaluate past performance and, if it meets the criteria, they can present it for assessment towards an NVQ;

- it provides a basis for valid and reliable assessment and stipulates what is to count as sufficient evidence of successful performance;

- it provides a basis for accountability in assessment.

A standardized method for classifying outcomes highlights what is common to different occupations and helps identify what is common within and between different occupations to be identified during the construction of new qualifications. This helps prevent artificial divisions between what are otherwise identical functions and enhances access to qualifications and mobility between occupations and jobs. It also helps qualification holders to transfer what they are competent at from one occupation or setting to another. Clear outcomes for assessment also underpin quality assurance.

THE NVQ FORMAT

The NCVQ 1991 *Guide to National Vocational Qualifications* states:

Assessment is a process of obtaining and judging evidence. In NVQs, the standards of success are *already* defined and are available to both the assessor and the candidate alike. Assessment decisions are a matter of judgement as to whether the standards have been met and whether the candidate has provided sufficient evidence to indicate that performance will be maintained in the future in the varied contexts defined by the range (NCVQ, 1991, p. 21).

Substituting *clearly* for *already* would better emphasize how important the format is for empowering the learner who can gain evidence outside formal education and training programmes and for providing a basis for reliable and valid assessment. The NVQ is made up of units, thus making it easier to collect evidence and accumulate credit towards an award. Units are divided into elements with performance criteria and statements of the range of contexts in which a candidate has to provide evidence of performance or evidence of the capacity to perform. Although I do not want to go into detail here about all components of an NVQ, there are some characteristics that I wish to draw your attention to:

- An element should be phrased so that it can be prefaced by, 'The candidate should be able to ...'
- Performance criteria specify the quality of the outcomes to be achieved and indicate how they are to be evaluated.

    Document 2.1 is an example of an element taken from a unit of competence for assessing NVQs and shows some of the things that an assessor has to do in the NVQ model. As can be seen, the element requires evidence that the candidate *is able* to 'agree and review a plan for assessment'. The other three elements that comprise the NVQ assessor unit require assessors to be able to collect and judge performance evidence against criteria; collect and judge knowledge evidence; and make assessment decisions and provide feedback to the candidate. These standards are an important part of NCVQ's quality assurance requirements. All assessors are required to prove their competence to assess NVQs by demonstrating that they have achieved the outcomes specified in the four elements.

    As can be seen, the performance criteria are a mixture of products and processes. They have to be assessable and, for that reason, it would not be acceptable to couch them in terms of 'know ...' or 'be aware of ...' or 'develop an understanding of ...'. Note that as with other performance criteria, criterion (h) states an *outcome* – 'the assessment plan' – and the way it is to be *evaluated* – 'specifies the target elements of competence, the types of evidence to be collected, the assessment methods, the timing of assessments and the arrangements for reviewing progress against the plan.'

Document 2.1   *An example of an NVQ unit taken from the National Standards for Assessment and Verification*

Unit: D32   Assess Candidate Performance

Element: D321   Agree and review a plan for assessing performance

Performance Criteria

a   the opportunities identified are relevant to the element to be assessed

b   best use is made of naturally occurring evidence and related questioning

c   opportunities are selected to minimise disruption to normal activity

d   opportunities are selected which provide access to fair and reliable assessment

e   when simulations are proposed, accurate information and advice is sought about their validity and administration

f   the proposed assessment plan is discussed and agreed with the candidate and others who may be affected

g   if there is disagreement with the proposed assessment plan, options open to the candidate are explained clearly and constructively

h   the assessment plan specifies the target elements of competence, the types of evidence to be collected, the assessment methods, the timing of assessments and the arrangements for reviewing progress against the plan

i   plans are reviewed and updated at agreed times to reflect the candidate's progress within the qualification

Range Statements

1   Evidence
Performance evidence; knowledge evidence

2   Evidence derived from
Examination of products; observations of process; responses to questions

3   Opportunities for evidence collection
Naturally occurring; pre-set simulations and tests;
For candidates with special assessment requirements

Evidence Requirements

The performance evidence required:
One assessment plan for one candidate covering at least three elements. The plan should be assessed by examining it (or a copy of it).

The knowledge evidence required:

i   ways of involving different candidates in developing and agreeing assessment plans to meet their needs;

ii what evidence requirements are, and how to identify relevant evidence from what is actually or potentially available;

iii what naturally occurring evidence is and why it is important for assessment purposes;

iv different methods for collecting performance evidence and how to select appropriate, efficient methods;

v   when to use simulations and alternative sources, and from whom to seek advice when simulations and alternative sources are required;

vi the place of knowledge evidence in assessment and ways of collecting it;

vii how to meet candidates' needs for access to fair and reliable assessment in line with the relevant legislation, and how to recognise and eliminate unfair discrimination;

viii what types of special assessment requirements there are, ways of providing for them and who to approach for advice.

- The range gives further information, where this is considered necessary, about the contexts in which elements and performance criteria are to apply.

  In Document 2.1, the range specifies the types of evidence that have to be covered, sources of evidence, and the opportunities for collecting the evidence. Note that this range includes 'knowledge', 'questions' and 'pre-set tests'. Before candidates are deemed to be competent, they will have to demonstrate that they can perform across all of the contexts listed in the range for this element.

- Finally there are the evidence requirements which specify what is to be counted as sufficient for assessment and which include knowledge and understanding.

Precision

In 1991 Gilbert Jessup wrote:

> There will be rules (criteria) governing the form of statements [the specifications of outcomes cited above]. These will be linguistic conventions to aid the communication on the meaning of statements. There are also what have been described as technical requirements to ensure that the statements meet the need for assessment, but this is simply another way of saying that *statements must accurately communicate their intent.* For accurate communication of the outcomes of competence and attainment, *a precision in the use of language in such statements will need to be established, approaching that of science. The overall model stands or falls on how effectively we can state competence and attainment* (p. 134, emphases added).

Almost four years on, this can be considered to be over-optimistic and to overstate the degree of precision that is possible, because:

- formulating precise rules to cover contingencies is very difficult. It is hard to get people to agree about wording in the NVQ format that will be clearly understood by candidates, employers, assessors and other users;

- more information has had to be introduced to make the meaning of NVQs clear, thus adding to the size of specifications and their complexity;

- despite the additions to the specifications, it is now widely recognized that the specifications have to be supplemented to ensure that assessment is reliable and valid.

There are what may be called 'political' problems. The more explicit one makes outcomes, the more likely it is that disagreements will arise between different interests. What has hitherto been conveniently covered over is now brought clearly into view (see also Chapter 1). The strength of the model is also a potential weakness.

The trend, predictably, has been to add information to meet criticisms that the original specifications were too general and would lead to unreliable and invalid assessment. For example, range statements were introduced to make clear the contexts which candidates were expected to cover either in the workplace, in a simulation, or by questioning or other methods. This was followed by the addition of evidence requirements including knowledge specifications. Document 2.1 contains examples of both range statements and of evidence requirements.

Given the importance attached to making outcomes explicit in order to empower learners, it is disappointing that there have been reports that people find the specifications difficult to read. However, these concerns may simply be short-term difficulties with an unfamiliar format which, with use, will disappear. We also need to compare like with like: the NVQ specifications fulfil the role of a range of documents setting the criteria for assessment for other qualifications. Unlike NVQs, these documents are not necessarily meant for those who are to be assessed. For example, I suggest that rough equivalencies could be made between an A level and an NVQ, as shown in Table 2.1. It would be interesting to know how those seeking the qualifications use any of these A level documents, if at all. All but the external verifier reports are designed for the NVQ candidate to see and use.

Of course, this comparison is not entirely fair because traditional A levels are based on unseen written examinations and the comparison should be made with similar types of qualifications involving a large amount of continuous assessment. Given the function of NVQs, comparison should be made with specifications that seek to assess behaviour and products in the workplace. Arguably, this form of assessment is not well developed and would benefit from the NVQ format. Eraut and Cole (1993) found wide variations in the quality of assessment instruments available to assessors carrying out workplace assessment in a sample of professions. While in the best cases it was possible for a complete outsider to recognize the validity of many measures employed, even though the degree of specificity and/or clarity varied between examples, in other cases the criteria were either too vague or there were no explicit criteria. They found that generally, the use of explicit assessment criteria in the workplace-based assessments contrasted poorly with their use in higher

Table 2.1 *A comparison between NVQs and A level specifications*

NVQs	A Levels
Range	
Evidence requirements	
Examples	Syllabus: including aims and objectives,
Guidance	and recommended texts
Units	Objectives *qua* outcomes
Elements	Examination papers
Performance criteria	Descriptions of practicals/simulations
External verifier reports	Marking schemes
	Examiners' reports

education contexts. This was likely to reduce the validity and reliability of workplace assessment and the public accountability of the qualification.

The late Harry Black and his colleagues evaluated the outcomes format used in SCOTVEC qualifications using similar specifications of outcomes to those used in NVQs (Black *et al.*, 1989). He also looked at the format for NVQs for staff in museums (Black, 1992). It is clear from his findings that to obtain reliable and valid assessments, even when the outcomes are explicit, requires examples/exemplars of good and bad assessment practices, the exercise of professional judgement, training and socialization of assessors, the building of case law, networking between assessors, and effective monitoring and reviewing of the assessment process. As always, quality assurance is based on a community of trained assessors and verifiers within a profession, working to clear and explicit standards.

Although NCVQ has introduced knowledge specifications and other evidence requirements, even these may not be sufficient:

> Evidence requirements are a vital aspect in the assessment process, but they cannot carry the whole system. Further support and guidance is still needed to help assessors evaluate the quality of evidence and implement the assessment scheme locally (Mitchell and Bartram, 1994, p. 39).

The architects of the NVQ model would, no doubt, agree that they underestimated the difficulties in making outcomes explicit. I do not think that anyone would any longer entertain the possibility that we can develop 'precision in the use of language approaching that of a science' although the pursuit of the holy grail of clear outcomes remains.

The place of NVQ specifications of outcomes is analogous in some ways to the place of law in the legal framework. Stanley Fish argues that the law is never free from interpretation no matter how abstract or particular it is but, despite this, it succeeds, 'although the nature of that success – it is a political/rhetorical achievement – renders it bitter to the formalist taste' (Fish, 1994, p. 144).

> ... the law is continually creating and recreating itself out of the very materials and forces it is obliged, by the very desire to *be* law, to push away. The result is a spectacle that could be described (as members of the critical legal studies movement tend to do) as farce, but I would describe it differently, as a signal example of the way in which individuals are able to construct the roadway on which they are travelling, even to the extent of 'demonstrating' in the course of building it that it was there all the while. The failure of legal positivists and natural law theorists to find a set of neutral procedures or

basic moral principles underlying the law should not be taken to mean that the law is a failure, but rather that it is an amazing kind of success (Fish, 1994, p. 156).

Knowledge

A certificate that indicates performance in a written examination which tests the ability to describe, to state facts or develop a logical argument is valuable but it is not a statement of competence that we would wish to have. Many existing vocational qualifications are of this type and most fail to give recognition to work-based learning. Likewise, a certificate that indicates the ability to exercise a skill or to perform a limited and sometimes artificial task is useful but it is not a statement of competence within our meaning. In satisfying the criteria for the National Vocational Qualification, accredited awards should not continue these deficiencies for most current certification (MSC and DES, 1986, pp. 32–3).

Knowledge has always been considered to be necessary for competent performance, although it has never been considered to be sufficient. The De Ville Review wanted more than tests of knowledge and skills based on simulations in professional qualifications. Work-based performance was to be the dominant part of NVQs. However, it became clear that more attention would have to be given to the role of knowledge in developing NVQs and to making it more visible in specifications. So, knowledge specifications – all of which must be covered by a candidate – and evidence specifications, which state what will count as sufficient evidence of competence, have been added to the NVQ specifications, as was seen in Document 2.1.

There are several reasons why these changes have taken place: to achieve greater consistency in assessment by making NVQ specifications more consistent and more informative; to establish whether similar functionally-based units or qualifications are truly identical; and in response to misconceptions about the role of knowledge in NVQs. Gilbert Jessup admitted that despite the appeal of the 'black box' approach of the early competence movement, knowledge could not be inferred simply from performance because it would be unrealistic to arrange for assessment to cover all of the contexts in which a competent person was expected to perform. In NVQs, though, candidates must demonstrate that they can perform in the contexts listed in the range.

It is also recognized that performance alone may not provide sufficient evidence that someone is competent. As Mitchell and Bartram (1994) explain:

Evidence from performance can sometimes be very unclear. Asking someone why they have done something usually reveals more about their competence than simply watching them do it. We may otherwise make incorrect assumptions about the reasons for their actions (p. 31).

They make it clear that knowledge and understanding can be used to improve and broaden the specification of standards and help identify critical outcomes of performance, detailed in performance criteria. They give an example from the development of standards for registered auditors by the Chartered Association of Certified Accountants:

During the development of the standards for Certified Accountants, there were insistent demands from practitioners and accountancy lecturers alike that auditors needed to know about the history of audits and what audits could, and could not achieve. After much discussion surrounding this issue, and persistent questioning as to how this would be apparent in, or would affect, practice, it became clear that many clients have unrealistic aims and hopes regarding audits – they think that they will achieve all kinds of things which are impossible from the history and use of audits. Auditors need to be able to explain the background of an audit to help clients understand why the audit is necessary for the regulatory purposes and the ways in which the audit can, and cannot, contribute to organisational performance. As the standards stood, the purpose and history of an audit could not be related to the performance criteria or statements of range.

An additional performance criterion was developed, related to the first meeting with a client. This was:

the purposes of an audit are explained in a manner and at a level and pace appropriate to the client and their level of understanding (Mitchell and Bartram, 1994, p. 13).

This example gives an insight into the negotiations about what goes into specifications and how the knowledge has to be justified by its importance to what someone has to do in an occupation.

So, the bodies that are responsible for the development of NVQs have to face the same problems as other bodies designing professional qualifications about what knowledge to put in, what to leave out and how it is to be assessed. Deciding exactly what to include may be difficult and deciding what to *exclude* may be even more difficult. Justification can often be found for the inclusion of knowledge, no matter how obscure it may be, and there is the countervailing danger of including too much knowledge. Among the problems associated with knowledge in professional qualifications are the following:

● deciding what is transferable;

● avoiding over- and under-specification;

● avoiding academic drift (not discussed here);

● deciding whom to consult.

Deciding what should be assessed to infer transferability

If someone demonstrates that they both know how to modify practices and procedures in specified contexts and/or that they understand the principles or theory which explain the nature of the function or activity to be assessed, then it may be safe to infer that they are competent to perform in these contexts.

In the glossary of his book, Jessup defines knowledge as:

the 'know-how' or cognitive component which underpins competence or attainment, which may include facts, theories, principles, conceptual frameworks etc. It subsumes 'understanding'. [It] may be elicited through questioning techniques (1991, p. 141).

Elsewhere in the same book he mentions the individual drawing on a 'repertoire of skill and knowledge' and he also devotes a chapter to core skills. These too are a basis of transfer as his definition in his glossary makes clear. Core skills are:

skills (or facets of skill) which underpin, and are common to, a wide range of competent performance. The acquisition of such skills is believed to facilitate transfer in a wide range of functions and situations (*ibid*, p. 140).

There are three things that could be used to infer the ability of someone to transfer between different contexts: 'know how', 'know that' or propositional knowledge, and cognitive or other transferable skills. There are dangers in taking any of them in isolation. Because they are always tied to performance in NVQs, that is they are applied, the danger of isolated assessment and the risk of drawing unreliable inferences are reduced. It may be appropriate to carry out separate assessments of whether theories and principles are understood as indicating the potential for transfer. Ultimately the candidates must demonstrate they could answer 'what if?' type questions and be able to explain why they would or did do something. Reflective practice has a significant part to play in NVQs as two of Mitchell and Bartram's five descriptions of the application of knowledge in NVQs indicate:

> Adapting knowledge and understanding to new situations to achieve the best possible solution/fit so that the outcome is the most appropriate for the circumstances ... where the individual has to balance the number of 'choice criteria' so that the best possible solution is arrived at.
>
> Interpreting new situations and phenomena, reflecting on meanings and deriving plans for action. Interpretation can be instant, rapid and deliberative (when there is time for thought after the event) (Mitchell and Bartram, 1994, p. 20).

Further evidence of how professional, transferable skills may be brought into NVQs is given by the Construction Industry Standing Conference (CISC) which has overall responsibility for developing standards for the industry. CISC has developed and approved a professional competence model although it has not yet been submitted to NCVQ for accreditation. This model includes units for communication, problem-solving, learning and advancing the body of knowledge and practice, client relations, ethical issues, independence criteria, and professional institutions and team work.

Decisions have to be taken about what need or need not be articulated by the candidate. Competence is a mixture of the unconscious as well as the conscious and the unarticulated as well as the articulated. It is useful to recall Ryle's well-known distinction between 'know that' – which would include many of the things listed in Jessup's definition of knowledge – and 'know how', which Ryle (1963) calls a 'disposition':

> but not a single-track disposition like a reflex or a habit. Its exercises are observances of rules or canons or the applications of criteria, but they are not tandem operations of theoretically avowing maxims and then putting them into practice. Further, its exercises can be overt or covert, deeds performed or deeds imagined (p. 46).
>
> The boxer, the surgeon, the poet and the salesman apply their special criteria in the performance of their special tasks, for they are trying to get things right; and they are appraised as clever, skilful, inspired or shrewd not for the ways in which they consider, *if they consider at all*, prescriptions for conducting their special performances, but for the ways in which they conduct those performances themselves (p. 48, emphasis added).

Finally, in deciding what performance to assess and what to rely on in lieu of performance, account will have to be taken of the level of difficulty and other characteristics of each context in which the professional will be expected to perform. Some contexts will be more critical than others for inferring the ability to transfer and this will inform both the structure of the NVQ range and evidence requirements.

Deciding on the degree of specificity

I shall illustrate the problem not with an NVQ but with an example suggested to me by a project on spreadsheet approaches to mathematical modelling directed by Alison Wolf and Ros Sutherland at the University of London Institute of Education. I am going to use a highly specific example which would not necessarily appear in this form as part of an NVQ. Take the example of a candidate in engineering who, as part of her work, is required to calculate the minimum amount of steel to make a tank of a given volume. She could use either a spreadsheet or differential calculus. There are overlaps in the concepts that she would need to know irrespective of which of these methods she uses, but knowing one method would not imply that she knew the other. Should the principle of calculating this kind of problem be stated and the method be left open? Should one or both be specified? Calculus may be the more robust or 'transferable' method but in practice the spreadsheet method will fit most cases. Plainly, this decision about the assessment of competence is not easily made – and will involve experts in revealing their values and beliefs about the nature of the professional activity.

Whom to consult?

Responsibility for developing and defining the standards for NVQs including the knowledge specifications, rests with a recognized lead body which should be led by employers, working with employees, and their education and training advisers. Mitchell and Bartram (1994) recommend lead bodies to collect information about knowledge and understanding from individuals within an occupation who are competent to practise, manage those who do, or who provide education and training to help individuals to achieve the standards.

LEARNING AND PROFESSIONAL DEVELOPMENT

NVQs are seen as providing a guarantee to employers that the individual can perform a job in a particular occupation, to the specified level of skill and competence (Department of Trade and Industry, 1994). Candidates will have to undergo a considerable amount of learning to achieve the competence to transfer to a wide range of real working contexts. They will have been aided by the ability to plan their programmes of learning with their mentors and assessors. However, NVQs do not specify what, if any, stages of learning someone should go through. Not prescribing how someone should learn has the advantage of allowing the autodidact who has learned in the course of doing a job to gain a NVQ, as well as someone instructed formally as part of a course. Ryle refers to the good surgeon who must have learned 'from instruction *or by his own inductions and observation*, a great number of truths; but he must also have learned by practice a great number of aptitudes' (1963, p. 49, emphasis added). NVQs give both learners and providers a great deal of choice of types of learning support and of styles of teaching.

It could be argued that NVQs should specify outcomes of learning that are not full competences. This could be an argument for 'foundation' type NVQs similar to Part One qualifications used in some professions. I shall briefly suggest why this might be advisable in some professions:

- NVQ elements are a collection of binary switches of 'not yet competent' or 'competent'. Candidates must meet all of the performance criteria across all contexts specified in the range and, in addition, demonstrate that they can apply the knowledge specified.

- NVQ levels are not identical to levels of learning as defined, for example, by Dreyfus and Dreyfus (1986). They identify levels of skill acquisition through which the trainee progresses to the intuitive judgements made by experienced professionals. These are novice, advanced beginner, competent, proficient, and expert. Although the Dreyfuses reserve the term competent for their middle level, NCVQ's definition of 'competence' corresponds, I suggest, to what they describe as 'expert'.

- To 'know that', to 'know how', or to 'do' are qualitatively as well as quantitatively different at the early levels of professional formation from the higher levels of professional development.

- The trainee in the early stages will learn by trial and error (and luck) in simulated exercises that are not rigorous enough to demonstrate competence. This style of learning is suitable for a significant number of people and it allows judgements to be made about progression to more demanding and more authentic contexts.

- The amount of time spent on these early stages of training is, for a significant number of people, likely to be considerable.

● In some occupations the public and colleagues need to be protected
  and the would-be professional needs to demonstrate they have
  reached a level of capability to *begin* to demonstrate their competence
  in real contexts.

If these propositions are correct, then a significant number of NVQ
candidates will be unlikely to achieve higher level NVQ units, let alone
receive certification, for some time after starting professional training.
The danger here is that standards may be lowered to accommodate
candidates who cannot demonstrate full competence for any or all of the
reasons that have just been rehearsed. However, I am not sure whether
this argument constitutes a strong case for national standards for the
early stages of professional development, including what Eraut and Cole
(1993) call 'capability', comprising the underpinning propositional
knowledge, personal skills and cognitive processes which constitute
professional thinking.

I want to end by referring to a recent project that demonstrated the
value of NVQ-type units in professional education and training in
universities. Challis and her colleagues at the University of Sheffield
(1993, 1994) designed a unit based on NVQ principles for an existing
module in general practice. Medical students took this option in their
final year; it included a short placement with a GP together with simulated tests. They concluded that the NVQ style of specification and
assessment was valuable in assessing work-based learning, the quality of
which was, up until then, variable. The unit helped provide better support for the candidate and made assessment clearer. There had been no
need to specify the knowledge required in any detail because these
medical students in their final year,

> have undergone a long period of observation, repetition and testing
> of content knowledge, involving facts, findings, concepts, theories,
> principles etc. of medicine in general and the specialities in which
> they have been tutored. They also have been consistently taught and
> tested on practical, situationally-specific knowledge through the
> observation of performance in a hospital environment.... It was
> therefore not the role of the general practice module to re-test these
> forms of knowledge. What it was important to test, however, was the
> students' ability to transfer their previously acquired knowledge to
> the new and very distinct environment of general practice (Challis *et
> al.*, 1994, p. 53).

The students, even at this stage, were considered to be 'advanced
beginners' or even 'novices' in terms of the competences for general

Practice. NVQs should be demanding qualifications if they are, as intended, based on the outcomes students will have to achieve as practising professionals.

Chapter 3

Assessing Competence – The Experience of the Enterprise in Higher Education Initiative

Sue Otter

AN INTRODUCTION TO ENTERPRISE

The Enterprise in Higher Education Initiative (EHE) was launched in 1987 by the Manpower Services Commission, later the Training Agency and now the Employment Department. The initiative injected some £58 million into a series of projects involving 63 universities, polytechnics and colleges of higher education. Each project was typically awarded around £1 million over a five-year period, subject to a satisfactory annual review of progress. While EHE funding was large in an absolute sense, it represented only 0.2 per cent of the total higher education expenditure and could have been regarded as marginal and insufficient on its own to promote radical change. Its attraction for the many institutions which bid for funding lay in the fact that it was not committed to specific budget headings and could be used as an incentive to promote teaching and learning development in a wide range of ways, at a time when general pressure to reduce unit costs, increase efficiency and student numbers was threatening to reduce quality.

The word 'enterprise' raised many eyebrows and provoked a predictable debate captured in inimitable style by Laurie Taylor in *The Times Higher Education Supplement* (13 May 1988):

How d'you mean – 'enterprise'?

Well, the simplest way to explain it is to use the words from the official document. 'Enterprise,' it says, 'is about effective and creative response to opportunity'.

That's it?

Oh no, there's more. It goes on to make matters even clearer. Yes,

here it is: 'Enterprise is a pattern of behaviour found in every aspect
of life.'

You certainly can't get much clearer than that.

In addressing the meaning of enterprise, higher education institutions
began to discuss the meaning and relevance of skills to the curriculum
and to working life; words like 'competence' entered the vocabulary of
higher education; descriptions of the often implicit qualities and attributes expected of graduates were produced; and programmes designed
to define, develop and assess the 'enterprising' qualities of students
blossomed. The strategy to leave institutions to define enterprise for
themselves enabled the development and design of programmes which
were appropriate to the history, missions and plans for the future of a
wide range of higher education institutions, and most importantly led to
the development of programmes with which they were comfortable, and
with which they would continue to work. The richly diverse initiatives
which emerged are described in the reports of individual institutions. A
review of the first 11 contracts was published in *Enterprise in Higher
Education – The First Eleven* (Employment Department, 1994) and evaluations of the whole initiative, undertaken by NFER (1991) and Segal,
Quince and Wicksteed (1994) give a flavour of the range of work. This
chapter concentrates on some of the enterprise developments in competence, focusing on the work of a small group of institutions which
chose to use enterprise to develop a model of competence that would
influence the curriculum of all undergraduate students.

UNDERSTANDING COMPETENCE – OUTCOMES AND ASSESSMENT

Historians of the competence movement might record that the enterprise initiative coincided with the emergence of the national occupational competence model which now dominates vocational education
through National Vocational Qualifications (NVQs) and General
National Vocational Qualifications (GNVQs). Awareness of the principle
of occupational competence has been slow to penetrate higher education, and although it is evident that those involved with enterprise have
been in the vanguard of interest, they have not been the first in higher
education to apply the principles, and there remains a suspicion in many
enterprise programmes that occupational competence is an inappropriate model to follow. The NVQ and GNVQ developments have,
however, had an important influence on thinking about the assessment
of competence. The two approaches to competence evolved indepen-

dently to meet different needs and, although fundamentally different in philosophy and organization, they share the principle of defining what learners are intended to achieve, rather than the courses or programmes of learning which are intended to develop them. Both are based on outcomes. The definition of outcomes can potentially have a fundamental effect on the assessment of competence; describing and making clear and public what the learner is intended to achieve changes the nature of assessment from a tutor-led system, with fuzzy objectives and undisclosed criteria, to a student-led system with greater emphasis on formative development and personal responsibility. Assessing competence effectively depends on defining and describing what the learner is intended to achieve, so the first step for many enterprise projects was to define and describe their competences. It quickly became evident that there was no shortage of candidates for the list of graduate enterprise competences; the problem was deciding what to exclude!

CORE SKILLS

The revitalization of core skills as components of the GNVQ and as a common core for vocational qualifications has had a further influence on developments in enterprise. Many of the enterprise competence descriptions borrow heavily from previous and existing core skill models, although some do not credit these origins. The NVQ core skills have emerged from work undertaken with SCAA (Schools Curriculum and Assessment Authority), the National Curriculum Council and the Further Education Unit, following initiatives by the CBI, TUC, HMI and others, and building on existing practice in BTEC, CPVE, RSA and elsewhere. These skills are intended to provide a national system for assessing and certificating attainment in core skills, and a 'bridge' between academic and vocational qualifications. Core skills units are available at five levels of attainment which are designed to link with the National Curriculum levels. The skill areas are:

- Communication*

- Application of number*

- Information technology*

- Personal skills – working with others

- Personal skills – improving own learning and performance

- Problem-solving.

(* required components of GNVQs)

The word 'skill' is emotive in higher education and complicated by a tendency to draw a distinction between education and training, and between academic and vocational purposes. Skills are thought to imply activities low in cognitive content that are typically learned through rote practice and therefore inappropriate in higher education. It is not surprising, therefore, that many enterprise projects chose to avoid the connotations of skills and to employ the term 'competence' to describe the attributes they sought to promote.

The notion of 'core', as an attempt to develop general and fundamental principles which will underpin all learning, seemed appropriate and several enterprise institutions have sought to promote their competence models as a core in this sense. The definition of 'core' in higher education is perhaps more concerned with the development of particular habits of mind or intellectual strategies, than with the achievement of readily definable skills which it might be assumed are a prerequisite for entry. Klemp (1977) describes the intra-personal skills of motivation and achievement as the most important habits of mind developed in higher education, and his work with Boyatzis (1982) identifies these as the most significant features of successful professionals in more than 200 jobs in the USA. These are plausible, even intellectually attractive candidates as core skills which can be developed in the cognitive context of different subject domains. There are, of course, other candidates and the definition of the common ingredients of competence in higher education remains open to reflection and empirical enquiry.

The ASSET approach to core skills

The ASSET (Accrediting Social Services Experience and Training) programme has been developed by Anglia Polytechnic University through a series of projects funded by the Employment Department. The initial programme was concerned with the development of a competence-based honours degree programme in social work. Subsequent work has progressed with Ford UK to a work-based programme in engineering for Ford company staff. The central theme of the work was the definition of a set of key criteria which would define the standard of the work. These were developed by a series of linked investigations entailing a combination of theoretical elaboration and empirical enquiry. The work, which is well documented in the literature (Winter, 1993b and Chapter 4, this volume), currently proposes that the key criteria developed in the study of social workers have considerable overlap with the criteria for engineers. The professional criteria, as they are described, are effectively core assessment criteria which apply to each learning outcome in each module.

The work is interesting and significant, both because the ASSET programme seeks to go beyond the simpler definitions of core towards the criteria which characterize professional, and by implication, graduate level work, and because its development and specification rest on well researched strategies. The criteria include:

- effective grasp of professional knowledge

- intellectual rigour and flexibility

- continuous professional learning

- task effectiveness

- effective communication

- interpersonal awareness

- commitment to professional values.

Each describes what must be demonstrated for the criterion to be recognized. The model is sufficiently broad to have potential as a generic tool, and further work planned will test its application on other professional areas.

Personal competences

The distinction between core and personal skills/competences is blurred in the literature and many of the descriptions of enterprise competences include personal skills in core skill models, while others seek to separate the cognitive skills from those relating to personal motivation and achievement and interpersonal interactions. It may be helpful to identify core skills in this context as a broad basic set of achievements, including cognitive skills like problem-solving and critical thinking, as well as communication, adaptability and working with others. Core skills are generally perceived as a required element of programmes with clearly stated levels of achievement.

Personal competences on the other hand do not have required levels of achievement: rather it is accepted that their development varies between individuals and is affected by their experience and opportunities and motivation for development. A model of personal competences developed by the Employment Department includes the following:

Making the most of what is done

- trying to make things better

- deciding what needs to be done and the order in which to do it
- looking at what has been done, looking at what was planned, finding out if they match.

Involving other people to get the best results

- identifying and responding to the needs of other people
- getting on well with other people
- getting people to work together
- getting people to see you in a positive way.

Managing yourself to get the best results

- showing a sense of purpose
- dealing with emotions and pressures
- being responsible for your own learning and development.

Using knowledge, skills and abilities to make the most of what is done

- identifying ideas and finding ways of using them
- getting information and making sense of it
- making decisions
- using situations
- deciding on values and working within these.

This model of 15 personal competences with accompanying indicators was derived originally from work on the Management Charter. Trials of this model have been held in schools, further education colleges, universities (Otter and Hadfield, 1992) and with employers.

Some enterprise projects have attempted to define their role in the university as providing all students with an understanding of the importance of core and personal skills within and beyond their university careers, as well as developing an understanding that the development of personal skills is both more idiosyncratic and significant in learners' future working lives. An underlying principle is that the university can equip students with the basics, as well as with the understanding that their future will provide opportunities to learn and develop, reflect and review and that the ability to continue to develop is one of the principal hallmarks of a graduate.

**EXAMPLES OF ENTERPRISE COMPETENCES –
WORKING WITH EMPLOYERS**

The competences adopted by enterprise projects have almost all emerged empirically, through debate, consultation and discussion. Unlike the standards methodology, which is a clearly stated route to the definition of occupational competence through standards which in turn become the qualifications of the NVQ framework, there is no evidence of an enterprise 'methodology'. Within individual institutions several approaches have been adopted, reflecting to some extent the history of the curriculum and local partners, and strong traditions of internal departmental autonomy. The following six, brief case studies show something of this range.

University of Teesside

Working with employers is a strong enterprise theme and one model of competence adopted by Teesside University is based directly on the competence model developed by the Ti-Oxide Company (part of ICI). This is far from empirically developed and resulted from a job competence assessment project using the McBer methodology. The theory of competence on which this is based is derived from the work of George Klemp and David McLelland and is described in detail in *The Competent Manager* (Boyatzis, 1982) and discussed by Winter (1991). A similar approach has been used to define the personal competences which are included in the senior management standards (M3) currently being trialled by the Management Charter Initiative. Competence is defined as 'an underlying characteristic of a person which results in effective or superior performance in a job' (Boyatzis, *op cit*). Competences relevant to particular jobs or families of jobs are derived through studies of people who are successful in that job. The competences do not define how someone carries out the specific functions of the job but they describe the underlying skills, qualities and ways of working which characterize people who are good at it (this has been described as 'meta-competence' by Fleming, 1991). Klemp (1977) suggests that such competences imply attitudes and habits of mind which permit the intelligent discernment of differences and similarities between one setting and another, together with the ability to modify and extend responses to the requirements of different situations. Self-confidence, perception and flexibility are the hallmarks of such competences. This methodology often results in competences grouped into three areas – cognitive, based on thought processes; interpersonal, based on interactions with others; and intra-personal, based on motivational factors. The Teesside model has 21 competences grouped in four areas:

- managing self (including prepared to accept criticism, takes on challenges)

- working with others (uses a personal theory to explain behaviour)

- influencing others (uses networks and contacts, shows concern to create specific impact)

- working to achieve results (sets clear goals, evaluates implications of different courses of action).

Coventry University

Coventry University also sought to use employers to develop and refine the capabilities which make up its Enterprise Code of Practice. Here a small group of local employers worked through debate and discussion to propose a set of seven capabilities:

- personal (including self-appraisal and taking responsibility for personal development)

- interpersonal (including communication skills)

- intra-personal (including working with others, accepting leadership when appropriate)

- vocational capabilities (including the appreciation of the values of work organizations)

- numerical (including the confident use of numerical techniques)

- information technology (including using computer-based systems)

- innovative and problem-solving (including transferring skills, demonstrating creativity).

The experience of one of the employers, the Rover Group, in developing programmes for young people as well as innovative programmes for young graduates and mentors was apparent in this work, as well as the experience of other companies (public and private sector) in management development, and staff training. The model represents an informed consensus view, subsequently refined by consultation with academic staff in the university. Each competence is qualified by a set of indicators which provide examples of its application in the university context.

De Montfort University

Other universities have adapted competences and skills from several sources to meet their needs. De Montfort University built on its experience of working with the BTEC Common Skills in several schools; on a pre-existing professional skills module offered across a large, combined studies programme; and on the Personal Competence Model (PCM) developed by the Employment Department (Otter and Hadfield, 1992).

This is very much a personal competence model in the style of the Teesside/McBer developments. It includes communication skills, which strictly speaking are defined elsewhere as core skills, rather than personal transferable skills; however the university took the line that since the intention is to create a working model which builds as far as possible on existing practice in the university these have been included in the personal competence model. Other core skills like numeracy and using information technology have been included as indicators within competence headings.

The model has four major headings:

- managing tasks and solving problems
- working with others
- communicating
- self awareness.

Each heading includes a number of separate *competences* which are numbered 1–12. Each competence is accompanied by a set of *indicators*, listed as bullet points.

Profiling at the University of North London

Other approaches to integrating competence into the curriculum have had different origins, the most notable of which is to promote profiling. Profiling personal competence is the basis of the University of North London enterprise programme, which is defined as 'a process which enables students/learners to articulate and, where appropriate, act on what they have learned, to review and reflect upon this learning, to record their achievements and communicate these to others'. The approach taken here prefers not to specify a model or list of competences and cites two reasons for this – the lack of a conceptual model on which the competences can be based and the difficulty in persuading some staff that personal competences are not objectively measurable characteristics of people. Each School is therefore left to define for itself the personal competences which are most appropriate for its curriculum content and teaching and learning strategies.

Oxford Brookes University

The enterprise project at Oxford Brookes University has centred on the development and implementation of a university-wide profiling system leading to a summative record of achievement. This system is intended to be introduced in 1995/6 for all students and has major implications for all aspects of the university curriculum as well as for teaching, learning and assessment. Oxford Brookes describes profiling as three linked activities:

- a process of reflection on learning
- the recording of significant learning achievements
- the identification of future learning goals.

It separates course- and field-based (Oxford Brookes uses this term to describe routes through its modular scheme) profiling, which relate to achievements on course, from personal profiling which can include anything a student does. The introduction of profiling and recording achievement has been marked by three steps: first an extensive process of consultation with academic staff, students and employers; second, and as a result of the first stage, the production of a series of documents designed to support and explain the processes and purposes of the scheme; and third a set of statements of student entitlement which describe what a student can expect at each stage of a course. All courses and modules are required to provide in detail the learning outcomes and skills which students are expected to achieve and these outcomes and skills must include a university-wide set of transferable skills – these include self-management, learning skills, communication, teamwork and problem-solving.

Sheffield University

Sheffield University introduced a Personal and Academic Development Profile (PADP) in 1992 as part of their enterprise programme. The PADP is described as a generic record of achievement and profiling system, with the aim of encouraging students to reflect on their experiences, identify their progress towards specified academic and personal goals and plan for future action. The personal goals include:

- use study skills
- handle information
- use information technology
- develop conceptual understanding
- analyse
- synthesize ideas and information
- use critical skills
- use methods of enquiry
- use practical skills
- apply theory to practice
- use numerical information
- communicate in writing
- communicate verbally
- solve problems
- work with others
- develop professionalism.

The academic goals are based on Bloom's taxonomy (1956) and provide criteria against which students can judge their ability to apply, analyse, synthesize and evaluate information. The PADP includes a student workbook designed to provide a basis for personal reflection and recording. This can be supported by academic staff in formal and informal settings.

UNDERSTANDING COMPETENCE – AN OVERVIEW

The distinction between core and personal skills and the meta-skill type of approach which enables an individual to adapt, select, adjust and apply skills in different situations, social contexts and cognitive domains (Fleming, 1991) is blurred in the literature, and many of the enterprise competence projects use what might properly be described as core skill models, while others seek to separate these from competences relating to personal motivation and achievement and interpersonal interactions. It may be helpful to see core skills in this context as a broad basic set of achievements, including cognitive skills like problem-solving and critical thinking as well as communication, adaptability and working with others. Personal skills are a refinement of some of these and their development varies between individuals and is affected by their experience and opportunities and motivation for development. The role of the university is to provide all students with an understanding of the importance of core and personal skills within and beyond their university careers, and the knowledge that the development of personal skills is both more idiosyncratic and significant in their future working lives. The university can equip students with the basics and, more importantly, with the understanding that their future will provide opportunities to learn and develop, reflect and review, and that the ability to continue to develop is one of the principal hallmarks of a graduate.

Enterprise has brought together several different approaches:

- the development of particular habits of mind or intellectual strategies
- core skills
- personal competences

in various ways. Some institutions have combined all three, while others have concentrated on one and yet others have sought to develop the processes of learning, reflection and recording, designed to develop competence, rather than define specific competences.

Problems with attempts to define and describe the intellectual core of higher education should not, however, distract from the reality of attainment of the students currently within the system and the very real difficulties that there are in demonstrating that they have all achieved mastery of the most basic core skills.

ASSESSING COMPETENCE

Staff and student attitudes

Understanding and agreeing the competences which 'enterprising' graduates might be expected to develop is only the first stage in ensuring that students develop them and are supported in doing so by appropriate methods of teaching, learning and assessment. Enterprise projects quickly discovered that even if academic departments were prepared to accept the enterprise competences, assessing them presented enormous challenges since it required an entirely different approach to teaching, learning and assessing.

A staff survey undertaken in one enterprise institution, prior to introducing an enterprise competence model illustrates some of the problems. The final report of the survey showed that the overwhelming majority of module leaders explicitly included such competences in their course documentation, but that there was some doubt as to the ways in which the competences were interpreted and assessed. Subsequent interviews with staff were directed specifically at this question. Respondents were asked if competence in personal transferable skills was assessed; the responses are shown in Table 3.1.

The report concluded that:

● the concept of personal transferable skills is generally well supported by staff

● a large proportion of course leaders believe that their courses go a considerable way to providing opportunities for students to develop these skills but about half of those interviewed did not specifically assess them

● a large number of staff expected their students to be proficient in these skills without giving them specific support

● proficiency in students is not developed to the level that staff believe

● staff do not feel that they have the time or expertise to develop these skills

● students find 'add on' skills modules unacceptable, particularly where they are not assessed and do not contribute to their overall classification

● students value personal transferable skills and have a clear understanding of their relevance in both the courses they were taking and in the job market.

One of the most significant problems was that staff thought it was not necessary to develop or assess personal competences explicitly. There appeared to be an assumption that competences developed as part of the

Table 3.1 *Assessment of competence in personal transferable skills*

NO	3
YES (but implicitly)	30
YES (specifically and implicitly)	24

higher education experience. In-depth interviews showed that in some cases this was founded on a genuine belief that it was not part of their, or the university's responsibility, while in others it reflected a real concern that to assess competences one had to be competent oneself, in much the same way as the assessment of knowledge relies on the expertise of the assessor. Many staff were intimidated by the lists of competences and declared themselves unable to assess students in these areas.

The difficulties illustrated by this survey are reflected in the ways in which enterprise projects have sought to ensure that assessment of competence becomes a real activity rather than a principle to which lip-service is paid.

Embedding competence in the curriculum

There were examples of competence-based assessment in higher education prior to enterprise funding. The majority of these were developments in individual departments, relating to particular courses or families of courses, and often initiated by small groups of staff or individuals. A number of enterprise developments followed this route, taking the principle of 'allowing a thousand flowers to bloom'; projects in individual departments were supported by small amounts of funding, and attempts made to transfer the ideas to other departments and faculties. The results were not always spectacularly successful since many of the projects related to specific vocational courses (education and engineering) and neither the competences nor form of assessment used transferred readily to other academic departments. Models used in teacher education were often well developed in many institutions (see Chapters 5 and 6 in this volume, for example), but attempts to transfer them without the philosophy of reflection on practice which underpinned education courses were often unsuccessful.

A further problem is evident from student responses to assessing competence. The evaluation of one university enterprise model of personal competence development showed that where it was a voluntary student activity, between 15 and 57 per cent of the students who completed evaluation questionnaires had used the materials provided, the majority only once. Students reported being unclear about the purpose and benefits of the programme. In addition, there was no correlation between use of the materials and either an introductory session or the level of tutor support. On the other hand students, staff, graduates and employers agreed that the principles of self-reflection and self-assessment encouraged by the materials were worthwhile and valuable. Students were further asked whether the developing personal competence could affect their learning in the long term and, even in electrical and electronic engineering where this was a compulsory part of a professional skills course, only 44 per cent of students thought it would have an effect on their learning.

The evaluation concluded that greater integration of the competence development programme into courses was required, together with support through tutorials. It recognized that academic tutorials were unlikely to be able to provide the level of support required and that staff needed to seek ways of using the materials developed by enterprise as a means of feedback mechanism for assessed work and as a means of encouraging peer student support through discussion. Overall it concluded that this might require relatively large amounts of tutor/student time and thought to make it work.

> If the main objective is to help students identify their strengths and weaknesses, there may be simpler, more efficient ways of doing this. If the main objective of the programme is to help students develop their skills, there is a need for more structured support for students.... At present findings from this study suggest we should proceed with some caution.[1]

Evaluations of other enterprise schemes have been undertaken, and although not always as extensive as this, they hint at similar findings. Unless the competences are integrated into modules and courses, they will not be recognized as having parity with other academic curriculum content and are unlikely to be taken seriously by staff and students. Embedding is a further prerequisite of assessing competence.

There are two approaches to embedding competence evident from enterprise projects. One is to use the processes of course validation and review to place a requirement on all courses or programmes of study to demonstrate how competences are developed and assessed. A university- or college-wide model of competence may be used, or Schools and departments may be required to develop models appropriate to their needs and to indicate both how the competences are developed through teaching and learning strategies and how they are assessed and recorded. The Coventry University Code of Practice is such an example. This was developed through enterprise and includes the capabilities listed in the previous section. All academic programmes at undergraduate level are required at course review and validation to provide a strategy for the implementation of the code. Since the undergraduate curriculum is modular, this is effectively achieved through the inclusion of enterprise capabilities in the mandatory modules which make up each student programme. Course teams are provided with a *Guide to the Enterprise Code of Practice* (Coventry University, 1994) which draws on projects in various departments to illustrate a range of approaches to assessment. The scheme will be implemented in the academic year 1994/5, and courses approaching review will be required to provide documentation on how they will support the development of the capabilities, how they will develop the vocational capabilities and how the vocational relevance of the course will be assured.

The De Montfort University personal transferable skills (PTS) model is integrated in a similar manner, and again utilizes the internal processes of quality assurance, in this case the course log, to ensure that all modules include, record and review actively their approach to developing and assessing competence, and its success in practice. At De Montfort a slightly different approach has been taken to assessment at the modular level and here the on-line module database will include details of those specific assessments which will provide evidence of the PTS. Students will undertake assessments which will provide evidence of academic achievement and contribute to module grades. The same work will also include evidence of the personal competences which will be recorded separately and not used for grading purposes. Students will be eligible to receive a separate certificate attesting to their achievement of the personal competences in addition to a degree transcript detailing the modules undertaken and passed.

The major alternative to this is the profiling approach which generally requires all modules or courses to state either all their learning outcomes, including skills and personal competences appropriate to each course or programme and not centrally defined, or requires the inclusion of details of how centrally defined competences will be integrated, developed and assessed.

Performance criteria and indicators of achievement

There are basically two ways in which institutions have chosen to assess enterprise competences. The first builds on some of the principles of the assessment of occupational competence. Here the inclusion of criteria which clearly state what a person must do to be recognized as competent is integral to the whole approach. NVQs use a sophisticated system of performance criteria and require candidates to provide evidence of these to prove their competence. Evidence is largely performance-based and therefore observable in a workplace setting; it is augmented by questioning and by other forms of testing which provide evidence of understanding and of alternative actions in more complex circumstances which may not be readily observed. Each NVQ unit of competence is divided into elements (each of which has performance criteria, the means by which a person can be recognized as competent) and range statements, which describe the contexts in which the competence must be demonstrated. Assessment is summative – candidates must meet the requirements of all the performance criteria and range statements to complete the element and unit. These are recognized on a 'yes or no' basis and no attempt is made to grade or to compare achievement. This does not require lots of separate assessment, but rather ensures that assessment is realistically based on the situations which occur in the workplace and encompasses all the variation inherent in it. This approach defines closely the evidence required, and permits less scope for interpretation on the part of an assessor. It seeks to ensure a reproducible standard of performance between candidates. The validity of the assessment is established by the standards of competence on which the units and elements are based. These are derived from work with the relevant employment sector and relate as closely as possible to real work situations. The reliability of the system is provided by a requirement for assessor training to national standards and by the use of verifiers (also trained) to ensure that assessment systems work properly.

The principle of occupational competence is intended to demonstrate unequivocally that the individual is competent to practise in a specified work role; this is clearly not the intention of many enterprise competence schemes. A degree, whether specifically vocational or not, attests to many diverse abilities, not just to competence in a specified role. One of its principal hallmarks is the development of attitudes and habits of mind which promote creativity, flexibility and individuality and it is these characteristics which enterprise schemes have sought to develop. The assessment of such competences is intended to promote their habitual use, rather than measure their achievement in specified settings. The use of criteria to assess enterprise competences tends therefore to be more flexible; there are rarely requirements that students demonstrate all the assessment criteria in several settings, and there is a general acceptance that competence will not be achieved during a student career but will develop and adapt over a working lifetime. Assessment tends to be formative, with the intention of developing awareness of the breadth of application of competences and the need to keep learning.

The formative assessment of competence finds greater application in the assessment of personal competences, where absolute achievement is secondary to encouraging continued development. It is the basis of much work in management development and uses indicators or examples of achievement which describe some or all of the types of activity which could be used to recognize the competence. Effectively it sets out what a competent person might do and asks the candidate to consider whether s/he does something similar. In contrast to the performance criteria used in NVQs, a personal competence may have a wide spectrum of indicators and there is generally no requirement to provide evidence of achievement of all of them, and greater scope for interpretation and the inclusion of new indicators by assessors and candidates. The validity of the approach depends on the extent to which the descriptions of competences capture real student behaviour, rather than setting ideal standards not achievable in the university setting. Deriving the indicators from a study of typical, or excellent (as in the McBer model), student behaviour is an important means of establishing the validity of the model. Reliability of assessor performance can be improved by group work between assessors to discuss and review evidence of competence, and by periodic reviews of assessor groups. This approach provides less reproducible levels of performance between students and is largely formative rather than summative.

Relationship between competences and grades

Embedding competence in the curriculum, rather then leaving it as a voluntary activity, is a move designed to ensure that staff and students take it seriously as a component of the curriculum. Efforts to ensure that competence is embedded in the teaching and learning activities can, however, be frustrated by student attitudes. Not surprisingly, students tend to ignore activities which do not contribute directly to grades and degree classifications, and as the evaluation of one programme above showed, students can clearly describe the benefits of developing competence, but at the same time fail to take advantage of programmes designed to achieve this. The reasons for this are complex – student attitudes are strongly influenced by the behaviour of staff and by their perceptions of what is important. Evaluations of various enterprise competence programmes show that mature students value competence development more than their younger counterparts.

The field trial of the Employment Department Personal Competence Model (Otter and Hadfield, 1992) showed that a substantial proportion of students treated their personal competence development programme as 'something they did for their tutor', rather than for themselves, in many cases completing their personal diaries the night before a tutorial meeting. Changing the attitudes of staff and students is a time-consuming process and however carefully the programme is developed, consulted on and implemented, there will be resistance and apathy in some quarters. This has led to attempts to go beyond the principle of embedding through course validation and review to making assessment of competence a requirement for completion of a module or course. In some cases this meant moving from a formative model of working to a summative assessment of what the student had achieved. Some enterprise schemes have gone as far as seeking to grade competence-based assessment, using 3 or 5 point scales, and to including grades in the overall assessment of modules. Grading personal competence is problematic and often highly subjective and such approaches in enterprise schemes are unusual. Other universities have sought to make the completion of competence-based assessment a requirement for completion of modules, but have retained the principle of formative rather than summative assessment. The act of undertaking the assessment, not the level of competence achieved, is assessed. Students attend skills sessions, sometimes integral within modules and sometimes delivered separately, and complete assessments which may involve personal reflection, perhaps a personal diary or log, or peer-assessed presentations or debates.

Efforts to require the assessment of enterprise competences provided the basis for debate on the current assessment and grading criteria. If demonstrating competence were to be a requirement to pass, would this be fair when other areas of academic knowledge were tested by examinations which allowed a choice of questions and permitted a good performance in one area to compensate for a poor performance in another? What about students who were academically very successful but whose personal competences, notably in communication, were poor? Should they be penalized?

Assessment strategies

Addressing ways of assessing competence has provided an important means of challenging traditional approaches to written graded assessment in many institutions. Assessing competence not only requires different ways of working, it asks questions about the amount and balance of current assessment – what is currently being assessed? What forms does this assessment take? Written? Oral? Summative? Formative? Graded? Pass/fail? Using peers or staff? In some institutions these have extended to how long do students spend doing assessed work? How long do staff spend marking it? What does it cost? as well as to questions of validity and reliability. In many enterprise projects developing ways of assessing competence has resulted in a review of current assessment methods and a more critical stance. The effect of increased numbers of students and student:staff ratios has not been insignificant either (Atkins *et al.*, 1993) and in some cases enterprise has provided a timely opportunity to rethink assessment strategies more generally.

Three approaches to resolving the problem of assessment have been adopted by enterprise institutions:

- A mandatory record of achievement, which includes a summative statement or profile of the enterprise competences, is a means of requiring students to take the development and achievement of competences seriously and can be used to develop an understanding of their relevance to employment. Using a record of achievement with a personal competence model to record progress in work placement is an example. This does not require students to meet an absolute standard of achievement but it does ensure that they undertake work to review, reflect and record their achievement.

- A compulsory skills/competence module which concentrates on the process of development and awareness-raising of skills and competences in a formative setting. Such modules may contribute credits to the completion of an award, but do not contribute grades to the classification of it. Attendance may be a requirement for completion and the award of a separate certificate may be an added incentive for students. Compulsory modules are not attractive to many institutions since they pose problems for devolved funding; the module is often provided centrally, sometimes by a non-teaching department and diverts funding from faculties and Schools. School- or faculty-based modules are however not uncommon and can provide a cost-effective means of delivering skills training using specialist staff.

- Some universities have preferred to develop a cross-programme profile of skills, where each module or part of the course can be audited to ensure that it provides one or more elements of the competence model. Students undertake assessed work for credit within their modules or courses and the same work contributes to the achievement of the competences. This again can be recognized as a separately certificated element of the programme.

The experience of working with personal competences in the curriculum

The majority of institutions with well-developed models of competence are still at an early stage of implementation; many are working in line with course review timetables and the introduction of personal competences will be staggered over several years. The results of some of the pilot surveys have been described previously, but there is as yet no large-scale evaluation. A parallel project – the field trial of the Employment Department Personal Competence Model (PCM) described earlier (Otter and Hadfield, 1992), provides some examples of the experiences of staff and students in working with personal competences.

The field trial involved eight higher education institutions: the sample included pre- and post-1992 universities and a small college of HE, and courses ranging from engineering, occupational therapy, pharmacy, humanities to theology. The aim of the trial was to look at how the competence model worked in practice and this involved questionnaires and interviews at various stages with staff, students and senior managers, as well as observation, reports and taped records of sessions with students.

The conclusions of the final report were that students were able to work successfully with the PCM in a variety of ways, in tutor-led groups, in small student groups, in one-to-one tutorials and independently. The field trial showed that many students were initially unfamiliar with the concept of personal competence and took some time to understand it and to be able to work with it.

Many students did not initially perceive the PCM as being relevant or important to their studies. The more successful field trials were in those institutions where students clearly understood that personal competences were an integral part of the HE curriculum.

The field trial showed that students used the model in more and less sophisticated ways. Some students went on to use the model as a tool for personal reflection and development, others used the model in a more limited way, relating it to particular pieces of work. A small number of students saw themselves as 'already competent', and thought the model would be more effectively used with school students, or with younger students generally. Some students reported difficulty in finding time to work with the PCM – this was less evidently a problem where the PCM was integrated into the curriculum and where it was supported by work with tutors.

The PCM was used both as an assessment and as a development tool by staff. There were drawbacks to both uses: the field trial shows that the development model requires more experience on the part of staff.

The use of the PCM as a means of formal assessment requires careful consideration by the course team of the context in which the competences are to be developed. Staff found that traditional assessment criteria were inappropriate in the assessment of personal competence, and needed time to work with concepts like the type and range of evidence of competence.

The field trial showed that a range of academic and non-academic staff were able to work successfully with students using the PCM. The most cost-effective models of implementation may involve non-academic staff, with clear support from course leaders and tutors. The trial further showed that junior members of staff, working without support, experienced considerable difficulty in motivating students.

Many staff and students assumed that personal competences developed as part of higher education. The project has been valuable in that it questions this assumption, provoking a greater awareness amongst staff and students of the need for ways of developing personal competences positively.

The level of institutional commitment to the development of personal competences was also an important factor in the success of the field trials. Overall senior management were committed to the importance of personal competence but were often vague about how this would be achieved and what it would cost.

There was evidence of a need for staff development in two areas: first in developing a wider understanding of the nature of personal competence and its relationship with occupational competence, NVQs, personal profiling and records of achievement and, second, in developing facilitation and counselling skills among academic staff and others involved in work on personal competences with students.

CONCLUSION

The EHE initiative undoubtedly stimulated a host of developments in universities, polytechnics and colleges. At a time when the government, through the National Council for Vocational Qualifications, was embarking on top-down developments in the assessment and promotion of occupational competence, EHE money was being used by higher education institutions to support their bottom-up experiments in developing and assessing competence. Something of this variety has been shown, although problems, not least with students' attitudes to the Personal Competences Model, remain and will be further explored in subsequent chapters.

NOTES

1. The source of this quotation is not given, since that would identify the university where the evaluation was carried out.

Chapter 4

The Assessment of Professional Competences: The Importance of General Criteria

Richard Winter

INTRODUCTION

Criticisms of competence-based higher education as the starting point for the ASSET (Social Work) programme

This chapter describes the use of a set of general assessment criteria in a competence-based degree in social work (the ASSET Programme – Accreditation and Support for Specified Expertise and Training) as an approach to some key difficulties in the model of competence-based education promoted by the National Council for Vocational Qualifications (NCVQ).

The underlying principles of competence-based education, as exemplified in the work of the NCVQ, would seem to have much to recommend themselves to those concerned with the education of professional practitioners. They suggest that we should (and can) derive curricula empirically, by consulting the practitioners themselves as to the practice requirements of professional work; that we should (and can) formulate educational objectives in terms of required professional outcomes ('competences') which can be used as criteria by assessors; and that candidates for qualifications should (and can) produce evidence of learning from their practice, without necessarily carrying out a prescribed assignment or attending any particular 'course'. In other words, NCVQ implicitly speaks to us of familiar and acceptable educational themes, such as curriculum relevance, precision and justice in assessment, increased access to educational opportunity, and a general 'learner-centredness', which is the very first emphasis in Gilbert Jessup's book on the work of NCVQ (Jessup, 1991, pp. 3–4).

Nevertheless, in spite of this apparently respectable educational basis for a competence-based approach to professional curricula, many academics have treated it with the utmost suspicion. One of the most widespread criticisms is that the lists of specific requirements are 'behaviourist' (Elliott, 1991, p. 123; Norris, 1991, p. 332) and 'atomistic' (Ashworth and Saxton, 1990, p. 11; Elliott, 1991, p. 119; Field, 1991, p. 50). This is also presented as a problem of 'reductionism' (Whitty and Wilmott, 1991, p. 317) as opposed to professional 'holism'. Field (1991) sums up the underlying worry when he describes 'competence based assessment' as 'the new Fordism of the education system', ie, as a method of analysis and organization in which the motive of managerial control 'narrows the scope of initiative and field of responsibility of each individual in her work' (p. 50). Ashworth and Saxton (1990) suggest that competence statements are intended always to refer to a single behavioural aspect of a task, and therefore cannot encompass such obviously important matters as 'maturity' (p. 16), 'critical thinking' (p. 17), 'group work' (p. 14), and 'complex skills' (p. 12) in general. Finally, Elliott claims that competence-based approaches lead to the denial of 'theoretical understanding as a basis for professional practice' (1991, p. 119) and of the ethical basis for professional work (p. 124). The culmination of this criticism was the report by Alan Smithers, who roundly condemned the lack of intellectual rigour and suggested that we should take note of French and German vocational education procedures which retain a strong element of conventional classroom teaching (Smithers, 1993, pp. 38–9).

Such criticisms of competence-based education were the starting point for the development of the ASSET Programme, which was conceived from the outset (in January 1990) as a project which would attempt to negotiate a model for work-based learning combining precision and holism and embodying both a concern for practice standards and a concern for educational processes. This has led the ASSET Programme to adopt procedures which, while accepting the educational values underlying some aspects of the work of NCVQ, nevertheless involve a substantial difference in emphasis and in format. This chapter describes the nature of these differences and argues for the advantages of the ASSET format. In particular, it focuses on the systematic incorporation of general assessment criteria alongside the specification of detailed practice requirements (ie, 'competence statements'). The argument is that this gives due weight to the educational aspects of the accreditation of learning and also allows the demonstration of practice competences to be clearly associated with assessment at a particular educational 'level'.

The ASSET Programme was funded by the Employment Department (Further and Higher Education Branch) for a total of four years. The first two years established a post-qualifying practice-based honours degree in social work, under the general aegis of the Central Council for Education and Training in Social Work (CCETSW) and involved a partnership between Anglia Polytechnic University and Essex Social Services Department. (During this stage of the work, ASSET stood for Accreditation of Social Services Expertise and Training.) The next phase involved a partnership between Anglia Polytechnic University and the Ford Motor Company and has led to the establishment of a work-based honours degree in automotive engineering, based initially on the model devised for the ASSET social work degree.

The central feature of the social work ASSET model is that its approach to assessment is two-dimensional (see Winter, 1994b), and it is in this way that it explicitly attempts to address the issues outlined in the opening paragraphs. Briefly, the ASSET model combines the use of

- detailed practice requirements derived from the analysis of the specific 'functions' which practitioners need to fulfil in the course of their work ('functional analysis')

- general role requirements embodying an analysis of the parameters of the professional role.

These two types of criteria are involved in every assessment decision, as described below. In order to clarify the significance of this feature of the ASSET model[1] the next section analyses the shortcomings of the 'orthodox' NCVQ model which presents practice 'standards' in terms of a single dimension, ie, the progressive subdivision of an abstract purpose into a multiplicity of concrete tasks.

ONE-DIMENSIONAL ASSESSMENT – THE MANAGERIAL SPECIFICATION OF 'STANDARDS'

The NCVQ approach to competence specification involves generating a simple logical hierarchy in which the 'Key Purpose' of an occupational area is 'disaggregated' step-by-step into detailed 'Performance Criteria' for each 'element of competence'.

Let us take, as a typical example, extracts from the document which presents the 'National Standards' for professional practitioners working in the area of Training and Development, produced by the Training and Development Lead Body (TDLB, 1991). The overall key purpose of the work as presented by TDLB is to develop human potential to assist organizations and individuals to achieve their objectives. This is divided into five areas, for example:

A.   Identify training and development needs

B.   Design training and development strategies and plans.

Each area is divided into two or three 'key roles'. For example (B) above is divided into:

B1.   Design organisation training and development strategies and plans

B2.   Design strategies to assist individuals and groups achieve their objectives.

Each key role is divided into between two and seven 'units of competence'; for example, B2 above is divided into five units, including:

B23.   Specify the resources needed to deliver programmes

B24.   Test, adapt and agree learning programme designs.

Each unit is then subdivided into several 'elements of competence'. Some of the elements in B24 include:

B241.   Identify and select strategies for testing learning programme designs

B242.   Test and assess learning programme designs

B243.   Adapt and agree learning programme designs

Finally, 'performance criteria' are given for each element. In the case of B242 these are as follows:

a)   adequate, accurate and timely briefings are given to appropriate people

b)   tests are administered within agreed timescales, plans and budgets

c)   accurate and reliable information is identified and accessed

d)   confidential information is stored securely and made available only to those who have a right to it

e)   data gathering, tests and assessment activities are administered in a manner which enhances and maintains the dignity of the individual

f)   assessments are fair and justifiable

g)   assessment reports are presented which accurately and coherently describe the methods and results of tests and the conclusions to be drawn about the design of the learning programme

h)   reports are stored securely and made available only to those who have a right to them.

The implication of the logical hierarchy format is that it should provide a mapping of an occupational area which is exhaustively complete, and which becomes more and more behaviourally precise as it subdivides an original abstraction into smaller and smaller components. I have argued elsewhere (Winter, 1992) that this approach risks falling into a simple philosophical misunderstanding: linguistic maps of experience are not systematic, but metaphoric, and are thus always open to interpretation. There can thus be no suggestion that documentation of this type might provide 'objective' standards, as the algorithmic format might otherwise seem to imply. The important thing to realize is that we are not 'measuring' anything (with all those aspirations to unambiguous preci-sion that are so appealingly embodied in the clock, the thermometer and the ruler). Rather, we are evaluating evidence, and much can be learned about 'sufficient' evidence, 'standards of proof' and other key concepts in this process from writers on jurisprudence (see, for example Twining, 1990, on the myth of the 'the perfect map').

The main points I wish to make at this stage in the argument are that this supposedly systematic document leads to assessment criteria which

●   are neither particularly precise nor particularly consistent

●   are more managerial than educational

●   give little help in indicating the educational level for which they are appropriate.

These points are elaborated below.

The term 'performance criteria' hints at behavioural/observable/ quantifiable evidence (and hence 'objective' measurement), but all it means in the NCVQ documentation is the inclusion of explicitly eva-luative terms or phrases (eg, 'accurate', 'timely', 'in a manner which enhances ... the dignity of the individual'). These evaluative terms can, of course, only be applied to actual situations by means of further judge-ments as to how they will be interpreted: what will count as an 'adequate' briefing? etc. Similar questions can also be raised about statements much higher in the logical hierarchy. For example we can easily convert an 'area' statement into the same syntactical form as a performance criterion, eg, 'Training and development needs are identified' and then ask 'What counts as a "need"?' and 'What counts as "identify"?' (A list? Any old list? An accurate list? A list plus rationale?) In other words, the logical hierarchy format does not create an objective measuring device but an orderly series of comments, which can be helpful to those who are already knowledgeable. If 'standards' documents like those of the TDLB are 'occupational maps', they are not like Ordnance Survey maps, but more like a regional Good Pubs Guide. Of course, some of the performance criteria are even less precise than others. In the example above, 'accurate' and 'reliable' have a technical aspect which might place them at one end of the scale of precision, while at the other end we would have such terms as 'adequate' and 'fair' which immediately open up a whole Pandora's box of further questions.

The list of criteria also varies in terms of the implied vocational role. At one end of this scale we might put criteria (e) and (f), which present candidates with complex ethical judgements and imply a large degree of discretion in the application of specialized bodies of knowledge. At the other end we have (d) and (h), which imply only obedience to simple workplace rules, and are less likely to specify the direct responsibilities of professional trainers (learning programme designers) than those of their receptionists or clerical administrators. In between, perhaps, we find (b), which implies a sort of 'middle manager' role. Why, we may ask, is there such an apparently obvious inconsistency, especially after such a massive analytical effort as the logical hierarchy seems to proclaim?

The reason is not hard to find. The performance criteria are not intended to comprise a unified educational 'standard' (a level of understanding, knowledge, and awareness) but a managerial standard, ie, a subset of the various dimensions in which an organization will wish to (or be required to) monitor its effectiveness, its efficiency, its profitability, its conformity to external legislation as well as to its own mission statement. From this (managerial) point of view inconsistencies in terms of educational requirements clearly do not matter.

Indeed, NCVQ argues that competence statements (its 'standards') have no necessary link with an educational level:

> One feature of the NVQ model is that units [of competence] are not assigned a fixed level within the levels framework. It is the qualification as a whole which carries level (Oates, 1994, p. 23).

The 'educational levels' framework of NCVQ ranges from work which is 'routine and predictable' to work which involves 'the application of... fundamental principles... substantial personal autonomy... and... responsibility for others' (NCVQ, 1991, pp. 17–18). The NCVQ levels framework is, as I have argued elsewhere (Winter, 1993a), an unsatisfactory document which implicitly assumes a link between cognitive achievement, levels of personal autonomy, and organizational responsibilities in an uncritical evocation of a social class hierarchy. Nevertheless, the sequence of NCVQ levels does represent an attempt to outline an educational progression, as well as a managerial hierarchy, even though one may not accept the parallelism between these two dimensions. It might therefore seem to be a strange feature of the NCVQ format that its competence statements remain outside its levels framework, and that the set of criteria we have just considered could be applied to assessing candidates' work within a vocational course which was the equivalent of an A level or of a higher degree.

The explanation, as I have suggested, is that within the NCVQ format 'standards' are not educational standards but, ultimately, managerial or 'quality control' standards. This means that they have no clear relationship with educational curricula: they are not, for example, 'objectives' or 'learning outcomes'. This feature of the NCVQ work is likely to create considerable confusion; the Further Education Unit , for example, in its current attempts to establish a credit framework, explicitly *does* wish to treat competence statements as learning outcomes and to associate each learning outcome with an educational level (see Wilson, 1993). In the context of this debate the model of competence assessment developed by the ASSET Programme would seem to have a clear contribution to make: the ASSET format does have a systematic linkage between statements referring to practice requirements ('standards' in the NCVQ sense) and educational criteria. The nature of this linkage will be described in the following section.

THE ASSET PROGRAMME – A TWO-DIMENSION PROCESS FOR EDUCATIONAL ASSESSMENT

The first process in establishing the competence statements which were to be the starting point for the ASSET social work degree was not the 'functional analysis' discussions with practitioners as to what their work involves. Instead, our first emphasis was to establish a general set of criteria which could be used to clarify the level at which the competences would be assessed, namely at the level of 'an honours degree' and at the level of 'professional' practice. In other words, we realized from the outset that it would be important for an educational curriculum document to resolve the difficulties previously noted, and which – even in 1990, when our work began – were apparent in the NCVQ approach (see Winter and Maisch, 1991).

Three separate studies[2] were therefore undertaken in order to establish the general criteria. These were as follows:

- a) An empirical study of the categories used by academic examiners in evaluating honours degree level work in a variety of different disciplines. These were at first taken to be specific to honours degree level study, but subsequent research showed that most of the categories used by examiners were common to all post-school study (see Winter, 1994a), so that what this study established should be described perhaps as 'characteristics of successful academic work'.

- b) An empirical study of the categories used by social work practitioners to indicate the qualities required for successful professional practice. This study used the Kelly Personal Construct Repertory Grid method of investigation and analysis – see Kelly, 1955.

- c) A theoretical study of the nature of the professional role, with particular reference to interpersonal professional work (eg, social work, teaching, management, etc.)

From the results of these three studies, a set of 'Core Assessment Criteria' was drawn up. These are presented in Document 4.1. They have been slightly modified (simplified) in the course of use within the Programme over the last three years.

In parallel with the work to establish the set of general criteria presented in Document 4.1, discussions with practitioners were conducted to gather data about the detailed practice requirements of their role. This work used the functional analysis method advocated by NCVQ (see Winter and Maisch, 1991) and led to the construction of units of competence which have much in common with NVQ documentation such as the TDLB 'standards' previously discussed. The main difference is that the general criteria were used to *exclude* from the list of competence statements any which seemed to be too 'simple' to offer an opportunity to demonstrate any of the general criteria. (This removes one of the difficulties with the TDLB example; see the comments on TDLB performance criteria (d) and (h) on p. 70 above).

The ASSET Programme competence statements follow the NVQ 'elements of competence' syntax, rather than the 'performance criteria' syntax. This simply involves making the candidate the implied subject of the sentence, which seems appropriate since the elements of competence are intentionally focused on the work of the individual, as befits a learning outcome within a curriculum document. The difference between the two syntactical forms is, however, in the end, a fairly superficial matter, such that one form of any given statement can easily be translated into the other. However, since my intention is to show the extent of the common ground between the ASSET Programme and the NCVQ format as well as the key differences, the example of an ASSET Programme unit of competence is quoted in Document 4.2 in a 'performance criteria' format, since it is the performance criteria which are

Document 4.1   *The ASSET programme core assessment criteria*

Note: All criteria must be implicitly demonstrated in the evidence for each element of competence in each unit : the evidence for each element must be explicitly related to one of the criteria; particular attention should be paid to criterion no. 1 throughout the work.

Criterion no. 1: commitment to professional values

Demonstrates understanding of and commitment to professional values in practice, through the implementation of anti-discriminatory/ anti-oppressive/anti-racist principles.

This involves demonstrating:

1) awareness of the need to counteract one's own tendency (both as a person and as a professional worker endowed with specific powers) to behave oppressively;

2) respect for dignity/diversity/privacy/autonomy.

Criterion no. 2: continuous professional learning

Demonstrates commitment to and capacity for reflection on practice, leading to progressive deepening of professional understanding.

This involves demonstrating:

1) willingness and capacity to learn from others, including clients/ supervisees/colleagues;

2) recognition that professional judgements are always open to question;

3) ability to engage in self-evaluation, recognising and analysing one's strengths and limitations.

Criterion no. 3: affective awareness

Demonstrates sensitivity to and understanding of the emotional complexity of particular situations.

This involves combining sensitivity with effective management of emotional responses in the course of professional relationships.

Criterion no. 4: effective communication

Demonstrates ability to communicate effectively in complex professional contexts.

This involves communicating in a form and manner which is clear, sensitive, and appropriately varied in style and medium according to particular audiences and purposes.

Criterion no. 5: executive effectiveness

Demonstrates ability to pursue the stages of a chosen approach in relation to a clearly established purpose.

This involves demonstrating decisiveness combined with sensitivity in making difficult judgements in response to complex situations.

Criterion no. 6: effective grasp of a wide range of professional knowledge

Demonstrates an understanding of the relationship between various types of professional knowledge, and an ability to apply this understanding effectively through practice.

This involves demonstrating:

1) comprehensive knowledge and critical evaluation of professional methods/policy/procedures; general theory/research findings; legislation;

2) ability to relate specific details to other contexts and to general principles.

Criterion no. 7: intellectual flexibility

Demonstrates an open-minded awareness of alternatives.

This involves demonstrating the ability to analyse issues in terms of dilemmas and/or to analyse situations in terms of continuous change.

used within the NCVQ model (like the ASSET unit elements) as the basis for the presentation of evidence.

The competence statements given in Document 4.2 suggest that, in spite of the criticisms quoted at the beginning of the chapter, competence statements can do justice to the complexity of the professional role, with its inevitable combination of the intellectual, the affective, and the ethical, its uncertainties and its dilemmas. Comparable examples in the context of teacher education are quoted by Whitty (1991, p. 10). There is no need to frame statements of competence within a narrowly behaviouristic, reductionist model of human activity, unless one is committed to a model of social enquiry which still has these characteristics (in spite of recent decades of development in social science methodology), or unless one is engaged not in curriculum design at all, but in articulating a format for managerial control (see Winter, 1989, pp. 186–93).

Document 4.2   *The social work ASSET programme (unit of competence 3): promoting clients' potential for independence (shown in NVQ performance criteria format)*

Elements of competence

a)   The full range of relevant resources and services and the criteria for their provision are communicated to clients.

b)   Clients are advised concerning the policies and statutory responsibilities of local authorities and the legal framework within which they operate.

c)   Clients are helped to recognise their own strengths and needs, and to assess and accept their individual starting points and capabilities.

d)   Differences between clients' perceptions and candidates' perceptions concerning achievable goals are understood, and a plan is constructed which accepts the outcomes of negotiated processes.

e)   Effective representations are made on behalf of clients.

f)   Supportive links are developed between the client, the client's personal network, relevant local organisations, and social work agencies.

g)   The theoretical basis for the social worker's authority, responsibilities, and methods of practice are understood.

h)   A professional relationship with clients is managed, in which the exercise of appropriate authority is balanced against an understanding of the necessity for client empowerment.

j)   Clients are involved in discussions and decisions which affect their situation.

k)   The relationship is clarified between candidates' feelings concerning the situation and those of the client.

Combining general and specific criteria

Within the ASSET Programme, candidates compile portfolios of work-based evidence and a supporting commentary to demonstrate that they have fulfilled the competence requirements and the general criteria. They begin by drawing up an action plan in which they consider how their actual (or potential) practice can link each of the competence statements (a–k; Document 4.2) with one or other of the core criteria (1–7; Document 4.1). This allows candidates a measure of autonomy in adapting the Programme documentation to the details of their own practice situation or work profile.

Thus, candidates might approach competence (a), 'the full range of relevant resources and services and the criteria for their provision is communicated to clients', in a number of ways:

- The obvious focus would be on core criterion 6, ensuring that the range of resources is very varied, detailed and comprehensive, and that the criteria for provision are explained in such detail that the principles underlying them are analysed.

- If this is a new or unusual type of client for the candidate, fulfilling competence a) may involve investigative work, which would then enable the candidate to focus their evidence on core criterion 2, 'Professional Learning'.

- If the client is one with whom communication is difficult, then fulfilment of this competence might also create evidence for core criterion 4, 'Effective Communication'.

- If there is a painful discrepancy between the client's perception of their needs and the availability of resources, then the fulfilment of this competence could also create evidence for criterion 3, 'Affective Awareness'.

What would not be acceptable within the Programme would be to simply pass on to the client an official pre-prepared document. This would fulfil the competence statement, but would *not* demonstrate any of the core criteria. It could be carried out by the team clerk, although the social worker might usually do this personally. In many cases it would be quite acceptable practice in terms of managerial 'quality' standards (and would thus be acceptable within the NVQ format) but it would not earn credit within the ASSET Programme.

It is not necessary to analyse all the possible permutations of competences and general criteria. Readers can do so for themselves simply by reading the competence statements (a–k) against each of the core criteria (1–7) in turn. Not all permutations make sense, of course, but there are always two or three realistic possibilities. Each combination of a specific competence and of a general criterion provides an intellectual and professional challenge and makes the demonstration of the competences a taxing educational process, while retaining the basic format of practice-based assessment evidence. I hope, therefore, that this example indicates the ways in which the combination of specific and general criteria enables ASSET Programme assessment procedures to ensure the level of the work is appropriate, both in terms of its professional quality (the value base of the work, affective awareness, executive effectiveness) and also of its intellectual qualities (the knowledge required, the ability to learn through practice, flexibility). This dichotomy (intellectual/professional) is, of course, not one which the Programme encourages: on the contrary, the essence of the core assessment criteria is that they identify the role requirements of candidates in a way, and at a level of abstraction, that leads to a synthesis of the practical and the academic, thereby transcending the intellectual/professional distinction. That, surely, is what a university competence-based vocational curriculum should aim to do.

CONCLUSION AND IMPLICATIONS

I have tried to show how the two-dimensional assessment process of the ASSET Programme can resolve the problems created by the NVQ one-dimensional approach. Single-dimensional assessment always runs up against Wittgenstein's problem of definitions: any rule-like statement apparently defining an action (eg, a statement of a competence requirement) always needs a further rule-like statement explaining how the first rule is to be applied in a particular context.

So, what will count as 'identifies' in the TDLB example? (see p. 68). What counts as 'the full range' or 'relevant' or 'communicated' in the ASSET example on page 73? This obviously leads to either an infinite regress or to a practical decision which ignores the problem (see Wittgenstein, 1963, pp. 39–49). Hence, all rules (and especially assessment procedures) can only operate as interpretive judgements within a knowledgeable community. Learning can never, therefore, be 'measured', as with a ruler.

Indeed, the limitations of the ruler as a metaphor for educational judgements return us to the alternative metaphor of the 'second dimension'. One of the few vivid memories I have of secondary school geometry is that the accurate way of identifying a particular point along a line was to construct a perpendicular to the line: the point is defined as an intersection. Rulers were excluded, with the explanation that each marker upon the ruler had its own irrelevant and distracting width, making 'accuracy' impossible. The mathematical principle here is that to identify a point along one dimension you need a second dimension; or, more generally: to identify a point in N dimensions, you always need N + 1 dimensions.

This is the principle underlying the role of the general assessment criteria within the ASSET Programme: they function as a necessary means for identifying a range of acceptable interpretations for statements describing specific competences. More generally, this may be taken as a formulation of the necessity for core or transferable skills in educational assessment, which is to be a set of *general* 'learning outcomes' operating as the requisite 'second dimension' in conjunction with the *specific* learning outcomes of a particular curriculum unit. As a principle for assessment it is also broadly applicable to academic as well as vocational courses, but this would require a further chapter; the work of Sue Otter on *Learning Outcomes in Higher Education* (Otter, 1992 and Chapter 3, this volume) would be a useful starting point for such an analysis.

NCVQ has begun to acknowledge the role of this second, general dimension of assessment in its references to 'communication, problem-solving, and personal skills' and it notes that 'the identification of such requirements may become essential' (NCVQ, 1991, p. 8). There are further hopeful signs in the GNVQ work on 'grading themes' which focuses on the candidate's ability to manage the learning process, ie, on planning, organizing, revising, selecting and evaluating resources, and self-evaluation (see BTEC, 1992, p. 14).

The ASSET Core Assessment Criteria document takes such thinking to its logical conclusion, and builds in the general dimension of assessment in such a way that it is not 'added on' but is inseparable from the specific, competence-based dimension. This, I have argued, is a way of reconnecting the specification of competences with professional values and with the challenge of a genuinely educational process. It might also be, as I have suggested, one way of beginning to address the vexed and vexing question of educational 'levels'.

Acknowledgements

The concepts, documents, and procedures of the social work ASSET Programme described in this chapter were developed jointly by Richard Winter and Maire Maisch, Social Work Training Officer with Essex Social Services and Senior Lecturer in Social Work at Anglia Polytechnic University. The Programme is a collaborative project undertaken jointly by Essex Social Services and Anglia Polytechnic University. The Ford ASSET Programme was directed by Samantha Guise, Learning From Experience, Anglia Polytechnic University. Both projects were funded by the Further and Higher Education Branch of the Department of Employment.

NOTES

1. The general criteria for the Ford ASSET Engineering degree are slightly different and they are used in a rather different way. This chapter focuses on the procedures of the Social Work degree. For further details of the Ford ASSET programme, contact Samantha Guise, Learning from Experience, Anglia Polytechnic University, Chelmsford, UK.

2. A full description of these studies may be found in Winter and Maisch, 1991 and Winter, 1994b.

Chapter 5

The Current Possibilities for Competence Profiling in Teacher Education

Peter Tomlinson and Sam Saunders

OVERVIEW

The teacher preparation sector of higher education currently stands in the midst of a veritable watershed of change, one of whose major strands is the UK government's introduction of competence profiling at both initial training and further professional development levels. In this chapter we try to stand back from this moving scene so as to assess the potential of the competence aspect of these developments. To do this, we first outline the nature of what has been proposed in the light of its immediate and longer-term historical contexts. We describe the rather negative initial reactions from many UK educationists to the notion of teaching competence profiling and the emergence of what we regard as more balanced perspectives, including our own attempt to apply relevant insights to the development of teaching competence profile practices within our own institution. We follow this by considering some evidence on the consequent effects and practices engendered so far across the new partnership arrangements between schools and higher education institutions (HEIs). Our final section will indicate some concerns and suggest broad tactics for realizing the positive potential of teaching competence profiling, while minimizing the negative.

WHAT'S HAPPENING AND WHERE HAS IT COME FROM?

The government's new arrangements for initial teacher education (ITE) in England and Wales have been outlined in two recent Department for Education circulars: 9/92 (DfE, 1992) for secondary phase teaching and 14/93 (DfE, 1993a) for the primary phase (so far the Northern Ireland equivalent is DENI, 1993 and the Scottish version SOED, 1993). The major features prescribed by the DfE for the new forms of ITE are that schools should play a much larger part than hitherto in ITE and that everyone concerned in such courses should focus on the teaching competences expected of newly qualified teachers. A more recent green paper (DfE, 1993b) makes it clear that the use of competence profiles will be strongly promoted. Circulars 9/92 and 14/93 offered somewhat differing formulations, but one of the last acts of the Council for the Accreditation of Teacher Education (CATE) before its demise in mid-1994 was to come up with a combined competence formulation for primary and secondary teaching and to propose that those completing initial training successfully should take their profiles with them into their first appointments and induction arrangements as newly qualified teachers (NQTs), and possibly beyond. At the time of writing (late 1994), the new Teacher Training Agency (TTA) is about to put out a version of this combined document for public consultation.

Importantly, the first of this sequence of documents, circular 9/92 (DfE, 1992a), made clear that its particular analysis and resulting list of competences constitutive of teaching was not to be seen as the sole, definitive model, but that 'it is recognised that institutions are developing their own competence-based approaches to the assessment of students' (paragraph 11). The indications are that this stance will continue: at a recent workshop on teaching competence, a DfE official indicated that the new combined model is very unlikely to be deployed 'prescriptively', though there is some uncertainty whether this relates just to formative/developmental profiles or also to summative ones.

Where has this competence emphasis come from? Its immediate provenance appears to have been the Conservative government's concern to 'tighten up' teacher preparation in various respects, the specification of the nature of the latter's 'product' being a typical expression of its market-place approach to life and in clear parallel to its outcome-oriented revision of education and training generally through the establishment of the National Council for Vocational Qualifications (NCVQ).

However, at further remove there lay a curricular approach with which the present shift appears to have more than a merely nominal link. This was the competency-based education (CBE) approach, which had waxed and waned a few decades back in North American teacher education (whence also CBTE; see Tuxworth, 1989; Wolf, 1994). This focused on learning outcomes and processes as the central concern of teaching and training, and stressed precision in the service of assessment and accountability. Unfortunately, it did this from the rather crude conceptual framework of the behaviourist psychology then dominant in North America, so that this competency-based approach paradoxically also became known as the 'performance-based' approach and was associated with specification of rigid procedure and artificially fragmented assessment.

More recently, Gilbert Jessup and his colleagues at the NCVQ have developed a more sophisticated and systematic learning outcome approach to training and education (cf. Jessup, 1991), which stresses the need for progressively more detailed functional analysis of occupational competences into units, elements, performance criteria and ranges of variation in context of application. In principle, at least, this approach appears to represent precision without behaviourism: far from specifying training procedure, for instance, it professes (cf. Jessup, 1991) agnosticism with respect to teaching/learning processes, but stresses instead the need for openness of access and the importance of assessing competence in realistic working contexts.

It should be noted, nevertheless, that although the same term 'competence' is central to the new DfE approach to teacher preparation and to earlier CBTE and current NCVQ approaches, the DfE not only makes no reference to either of the latter, but its formulations clearly do not utilize any of the NCVQ's more detailed concepts and terminology (see Chapter 2, this volume). Thus, for instance, the secondary teaching competence formulation of circular 9/92 had two levels, with five main areas including within them a total of 27 more specific competence statements. But the latter were still relatively general, including, for instance, the requirements that newly qualified teachers should be able to: 'employ a range of teaching strategies appropriate to the age, ability and attainment level of pupils' (2.3.4), 'decide when teaching the whole class, groups, pairs, or individuals is appropriate for particular learning purposes' (2.4.1), and 'maintain pupils' interest and motivation' (2.4.4). The most recent versions are still framed at this relatively general level.

HOW HAVE EDUCATIONISTS REACTED TO THIS COMPETENCE EMPHASIS?

If by educationists we mean those who write about educational issues in learned and professional journals and gather to discuss them at conferences then, as Rob Halsall points out in the next chapter, initial reactions have tended to be rather negative. The DfE stance has often been lumped together with the earlier CBTE and current NVQ approaches and attacked for its crude atomization of the organic whole of teaching into fragments which are not only unconnected, but put forward as mindless procedures, when, it is argued, they should be seen as intelligently adapted aspects of a contextualized and integrated whole (cf. Elliott, 1991; Hyland, 1993; Jones and Moore, 1993; Norris, 1991). Going still further, some writers, particularly those in the Stenhousian tradition such as John Elliott (1991), appear to see any attempt to be precise about what one is intending to promote through a systematic educational or training experience as a case of *predicting* outcomes on the basis of some sort of determinism. Others such as Hyland (1993) have joined him in suggesting that recent ideas on the nature of expertise and educational approaches focusing on the effective strategies used by experts would provide an alternative and better grounded approach. Still others wonder how far explicit statements will ever be able to cover all that is involved in teaching.

These sorts of reaction seem to have been echoed formally and informally at least at various types of educational gatherings and conferences we ourselves have attended over the last few years and, as far as we can tell, particularly amongst 'old university' department of education staffs, whose practices had on the whole apparently not included such precise course goal specification (consistent, perhaps, with the government's feeling the need for explicit pressure in that direction). Indeed, a recent study of teacher educator thinking by one of us a couple of years back (Tomlinson and Swift, 1992) concluded that in the UK this thinking tended – at least at the discourse level – to be characterized by something of a split between relatively broad matters of principle on the one hand, and relatively specific matters of practical detail on the other. We return to this apparent dualism below.

It must also be mentioned, however, that other educationists such as Furlong (1992), while remaining cautious, have pointed out that the broad competence formulations of the DfE admit of varying types of interpretation, broad as well as narrow. Recently, moreover, journal articles have begun to appear which resist the above 'demonologizing' trend by venturing beyond the crude all-or-none approach into more detailed consideration of the difficult issues characterizing the competence specification domain (though it may be noteworthy that so far it is not the UK that has spawned such contributions – cf. Gonczi, 1994; Hager, 1994).

THE NATURE OF THE ISSUES

The issues involved in the use of competence specifications and profiling in ITE are a large and faithful echo of the perennial, basic ones involved in the very notions of education and training. Thus the difficulties in this field seem due not just to their sheer number, nor just to the subtlety and complexity of the sub-issues involved, but also to their interconnectedness – not to mention that those wishing to get to grips with them do not tend to start from well-cleared ground, but from the ruts of existing conceptions and the track-marks of traditional polarizations, many of which we see as unhelpful at best.

We suggest that many of the battles in this area stem from confusions of two central, interrelated types. One kind stems from the absence of a relatively adequate, well-grounded understanding of the range and nature of human capabilities, teaching included. The other is apparent confusion – or at least a failure of application – with respect to certain relevant, but perennial distinctions. We would argue that such confusions have in varying degrees characterized contributions of both protagonists and critics of competence-based approaches and that in this area, even when people do appear to get things right in principle or at a general level of critique, they do not necessarily carry such insights into their practices or their treatment of further levels of detail.

These points have been developed at some length in Tomlinson (1995a and b). Suffice it here to agree with writers like Elliott and Hyland that our understanding of human competence may be illuminated by recent work on expertise such as that by Dreyfus and Dreyfus (1986) or Bereiter and Scardamalia (1993), but also to point out that there has been a whole tradition of cognitive psychological study of the nature of skill and its acquisition lying behind this work (and which in our view should have informed educational thinking and pedagogy long since – see for instance Gellatly, 1986; Tomlinson, 1981, 1992, 1995c).

This work allows us, for example, to distinguish a very important dimension of *openness-closedness* amongst skills. Here *closed* means relative predictability and clearcutness of context and goal, whence the possibility of relatively straightforward learning and training through demonstration and practice-based consolidation of 'sure-fire' procedures. *Open* means relative unpredictability and 'messiness', and typically complexity of context and goal, whence relative subtlety and 'invisibility' of learning, and difficulty of training and 'proceduralization'.

But even open skills, like all skills, are purposeful: they involve goals. To indicate in advance what one wants a learner to become able to do, is therefore to indicate the nature of the competence one wishes to promote and thus the goal of one's teaching or training. This is *not* the same thing as specifying the strategies or processes embodied in the competence, nor is it to indicate ways in which such strategic skill might be learned or taught. Nevertheless, even in the case of relatively open skills, a functional analysis, in which one seeks to analyse the constituent requirements, the necessary features of the competence, may be particularly useful as one basis for deciding with what one will attempt to equip one's trainees by way of strategy for their role. We would see this argument applying no less to teaching, though one has to add that in addition to the openness and complexity of teaching, its second-order nature (ie, its being by definition an activity that seeks to promote capability in other activities) does, of course, make it that much more difficult to conceptualize (cf. Tomlinson, 1995c).

When it comes to perennial distinctions which might inform this domain, one which was implicit in the previous paragraph was that between means and ends. Knowing what we want to achieve by way of learning gain, whether in school pupils or in learner teachers, by no means implies that we are claiming to know how to achieve such developments. Behavioural-type statements as sometimes seen in the objectives approach to curriculum ('on completing the course the learner will...') may indeed neglect this distinction and imply an underlying deterministic hubris (namely that 'we have ways of making sure that you learn successfully'). But on the other hand, to reject any prior specification of intended learning goals would be throwing out the purpose baby with the behaviourist bath water. It would mean, for instance, that we were entrusting *everything* (since the course is surely in the service of its outcomes) to intuition and practice – something that hardly sits well with the traditional emphasis in the university sector on an intelligent, thinking approach to life (let alone its recent emphasis under the Schönian banner of reflectivity).

On the other hand, it must also be said that to expect that *everything* about teaching could be itemized and articulated would be to neglect the very solid evidence from the experimental cognitive psychology of skill and its obverse, human error, that a great deal of the rich processing of information that goes on in truly skilful, expert activity is conducted tacitly and intuitively as what Argyris and Schön (1974) called 'knowledge-in-action' (cf. Dixon, 1988; Reason, 1990). This is relevant to another aspect of the whole teacher preparation and certification exercise and to a further perennial distinction, namely that between conceptions ('what we mean by x') and assessment operations ('how we tell that x is present'). To pin down functions to be achieved is not yet to indicate specific forms of evidence for these. Conversely, the possibility of indicating particular forms of evidence for a particular aspect of teaching competence must not lead us to think that we have thereby fully exhausted the possible forms such competence may take: course goals and their assessment may rightly drive teacher training course activities, but not rigidly and concretely. The intuitive nature of skilful activity referred to above may also be seen as relevant to assessment and the limits of course goal articulation. That is, as is typical in skill, those who are capable assessors, particularly of something as complex and open as teaching, can be expected to be able to 'do (by way of judgement) more than they can say' – a point that could also be made, as Richard Winter has in the previous chapter, on the basis of Wittgensteinian notions about the limits of articulation of particular forms of life.

It might be added, nevertheless, that this is no reason to cease our efforts to articulate as much as possible, at the very least for the sake of communication in the service of intelligent training strategy. This is the stronger line taken by Jessup (1991) and, accordingly, the NVQ approach includes attempts to specify not only the content elements of competence, but also performance criteria and levels, as also context variation through their 'range statements'. The contrast between the DfE approach and that of the NCVQ is particularly strong on this point. Whatever the underlying reason, the DfE appears to have gone for a 'British compromise' whose most detailed specifications of teaching competence aspects may total more than 20 in number, but remain relatively generic. Moreover, by indicating only that such aspects of competence need to be possessed at a level 'appropriate for a beginning teacher' and not specifying even types of context (eg, types of pupil), still less levels of proficiency at which successfully teaching capability is to be required, the DfE appears to be recognizing the role of experience and intuition in the assessment aspect of teacher certification. This in turn raises questions of quality control to which we will return later.

PRINCIPLES FOR DESIGN AND USE OF COMPETENCE SPECIFICATIONS IN TEACHER PREPARATION

Since life is never just a question of what not to do, but always of what actually to try and on what basis, we ought if possible to draw positive lessons from the sorts of resources we earlier identified as missing from the teaching competence debate. This sentiment is if anything strengthened by the realization on the one hand that the DfE appears committed to promoting the use of teaching competence profiling anyway, while on the other it still seems to be leaving considerable freedom in the detailed realization of such an approach. So we now want to suggest some principles for this domain, illustrating them through their application to the design of a teaching competence profiling approach with which we have been involved at the University of Leeds.

The concept of competence as capacity requires continued emphasis

Although the DfE and NCVQ approaches do not appear to fall into the behaviourism associated with traditional CBTE, nevertheless there may be a need to guard against treating competence statements as referring to the performance of teaching behaviours. Although any form of skill must involve within it the capacity to execute appropriate strategies, what eventually makes the performers' actions skilful is that the performers apply such strategies when appropriate, which also means reading the context intelligently and selecting optimal strategies, as well as executing these with an ongoing sensitivity to context (however intuitively these aspects may be achieved). This means that one needs evidence both of consistency and intelligence of achievement of the competence in question. In the case of teaching, exposure to profiling using the more simplistic notion of a record of achievement (RoA) may make insistence on the capacity aspect of competence all the more important.

Competence formulations need to embody the multi-level, embedded nature of teaching

There are clearly disadvantages to both of the traditional extremes in this area, namely vague under-specification and 'million tick-box' over-specification. If teaching competence profiles are to live up to their claimed promise of making assessment and certification more rigorous and consistent and of helping student-teachers and their mentors to manage better and more accountably the processes of acquiring them, then they must not only avoid such traditional extremes, but use what we know about the typically multi-layered nature of skill. Explicitly portraying the way that specific tactics are embedded within particular strategies within particular aspects of teaching should allow participants in training and assessment to give appropriate weighting to the various levels of detail in relation to each other.

For instance, one may need to specify particular types of class management function and sub-functions, and possibly a range of strategies relevant to these. One may also need to deal in terms of the central teaching function of the promotion of learning gains, its sub-functions and strategies. But in competent teaching both of these are not merely separately present, they are combined in an interrelated way, so that there needs to be some sort of reference to the integration of such sub-aspects in a teaching competence profile.

Another aspect of the analysis of teaching skill – for that is what a competence profile is claiming to offer – is the distinction just implied between functions and strategies. Functions are what the capability *has* in some sense to involve: teaching has for instance to involve awareness of the current state of affairs regarding learner progress, actions that engage the activity of learners, that assist learning, and so on. Strategies and sub-strategies are what the teacher actually *does* to achieve their functions and sub-functions. But one doesn't achieve each function through a particular, separate strategic action. There can be alternative ways of achieving the same teaching goal or sub-goal. Indeed, the notion is well established that different teaching strategies may need to be matched to differentiated learner needs. Moreover, strategies tend to be multi-purpose: the really skilful teacher is one who can deploy economical, multifunctional strategies which achieve many things at the same time.

Thus the intelligent formulation and deployment of teaching profiles requires us to take at least these two general features of human capability into account, namely hierarchical embeddedness and the function-strategy distinction. So, we must ask how the profile portrays aspects and sub-aspects of competence and how it is sensitive to the awareness and understanding possessed by those using it.

Teaching competence profiling should be characterized by pluralism within consistency

Although the move towards the use of teaching competence specifications and profiles may be supported by reference to the advantages claimed earlier, the above requirements for the realization of this potential can be extended to another implied by the same background considerations. In a variety of respects the use of competence specifications should be characterized by pluralism, although this pluralism must have some degree of consistency and coherence.

From the open and complex nature of teaching skill; from the distinction between teaching functions and strategies; from the embedded nature of all these; and from the variations in pupils and context typically faced by teachers, it is clear that anyone claiming to have analysed *the* one and only structure of teaching skill would be making not only a risky, but also a dangerous claim. Some sort of awareness of this doubtless informed the scepticism that greeted the task analysis approach offered to pedagogues by (then) behaviourist psychologists such as Robert M Gagné (1965).

Rejecting the idea that *one* such analysis can cover all possibilities does not, however, warrant rejecting the usefulness of *any* such analysis, particularly when one distinguishes between a functional or logical breakdown of what needs to be achieved and a strategic or psychological analysis of the actions likely to achieve it. Rather it suggests that people designing and using tools such as competence profiles should do so intelligently, which includes being informed by an awareness that whatever they do is likely to have some sort of limitation and hence relying on their tools only in proportion to the critical grounding available.

More positively, therefore, this suggests various sorts of 'pluralism within consistency'. A first is that, other things equal, the DfE ought to continue to allow variety of actual profiles, whether formative or summative. What one might apparently stand to gain from the alternative, convergent strategy by way of wide efficiency of communication and common standards could easily be outweighed by the effects of the imperfections of a sole template being multiplied by decree. We certainly should not go down any such route without clear consultation *and* expertly resourced working groups *and* considerable trialling and evaluation. To prescribe a single model without this would be to continue a present situation in which CATE and the DfE have simply come up with particular formulations (still containing quite puzzling phrases like 'subject application'), then simply sampled broad opinion and judged it in private. Continuing to do this rather than engaging in any systematic empirical trialling would surely be as arrogant a stance as ever characterized English amateurism in the educational realm!

However, it is hardly worth attempting explicit analysis without insisting that one's best efforts be taken into account by those operating in the field. Particularly if the DfE or TTA do go in for the sort of systematic research and development just advocated, and on condition that they enable and accept well-validated feedback from users, then surely it is only logical that the TTA should require as a condition of course approval at least that particular ITE training providers show that their competence approaches cover at least the aspects involved in the DfE's template, even if they do so using a very different carve-up of teaching aspects. We will return to this below.

Another sort of pluralism implied by the open-complex nature of teaching artistry concerns student-teacher learning routes. Just as an open-complex skill typically has a rich set of interrelated functions and embedded sub-functions, the whole admitting of many forms of strategic achievement, so the more complex and open a capability, the more ways of approaching and improving at the skill in question. This certainly applies to teaching, as narrative studies of teacher development attest (cf. Kelchtermans, 1993). The implication is that provided it maintained the above pluralism within consistent formulation, the DfE would be right to continue its outcome-oriented emphasis. Course approval may well concern itself with the appropriateness of provision for enabling the acquisition of such competence, but there should also be pluralism with respect to the very many forms in which this might be achieved.

Competence profiling is only one aspect of teacher preparation and needs to be informed by a well-grounded pedagogy of student-teacher learning

This last of our suggested principles has been implied at various points so far, but bears making explicit. We have argued that, subject to the above sorts of qualifications, explicit specification of the nature of teaching capabilities required for teacher certification is an appropriate and potentially useful function for an education system to lay down and for all involved in teacher preparation to utilize. But indicating the required outcomes of teacher preparation neither affects its mode directly, nor the particular parts competence profiles might play in the process. As with other educational matters, discussion of the pros and cons of explicit competence formulations prompts us to point out a need which actually existed independently and in advance of this development, namely a need for explicit reflection and communication amongst teacher educators regarding their own professional pedagogies and practices.

In this connection it is perhaps ironic (though hardly surprising, given what is known about the general human predilection for tacit procedure – cf. Reason, 1990 – and the particular love of taken-for-granted 'common sense' in English culture) that teacher-educators' outlooks have been far less investigated in comparison with teacher thinking over the last couple of decades, but that when they have been, the results have been no more encouraging (Mansfield, 1986; Tomlinson and Swift, 1992; Zeichner and Tabachnik, 1982). The suggestion is that the tradition of higher education, with its differences of resources and culture from those of schools, may well have allowed teacher educators in the university departments of education and in the colleges to preach reflectivity to their schoolteacher colleagues while falsely taking their own for granted. We have our suspicions that this state of affairs was partly (but only partly) to blame for the low esteem in which teachers often held their training and helped provide a hostage to the simplism of the right-wing lobbyists of government.

In any event, however, the point here is that teacher education could never afford such unreflectiveness and certainly cannot now in the context of competence profiling. A lack of pedagogical insight and intelligent adaptation in the deployment of competence profiling could indeed take us back to the rigid pathologies of the earlier era of CBTE. Given the current conversion into teacher educators of large numbers of schoolteachers whose under-resourcing and increasingly over-stressed experience to date has if anything systematically undermined their reflectivity, this point bears very serious consideration when thinking about the possibilities for competence profiling in particular and school-based ITE in general. However, having ourselves preached thus, we ought now to illustrate how we have sought to apply these views in our own practice.

THE LUSSP COMPETENCE PROFILING APPROACH

An attempt was made to embody the above points in the approach to teaching competence profiling developed as part of the Leeds University Secondary School Partnership (LUSSP) between the University's School of Education and some 45 local secondary schools. This was developed during Autumn 1992 and briefly trialled during the Spring of 1993 for introduction in our mentor development programme during Summer 1993 and more widespread evaluation during the first year of the LUSSP scheme.

It was felt that the DfE secondary competence statements in circular 9/ 92 were lacking in various respects, including some confusion of levels and a lack of connection with the actual cycle of events in teaching. Our alternative approach therefore analysed teaching competence hierarchically into four levels, of which the first three are shown in Figure 5.1. In addition to the *Overall Teaching Competence* level, the five *Main Areas* of teaching this comprises and the twelve *Sub-areas* of teaching seen in Figure 5.1, there is also a *Further Detail* level within each sub-area, which we have omitted.

The scheme involved four types of documentation:

(a) Competence Recording Profiles
These are seven-page booklets with boxed areas for written comments on each sub-area and on overall teaching, which come in three colour-coded versions, namely: a *Working Profile* without assessment scales, intended for informal student and tutor use of all sorts, and the two formal records, the *Interim Assessment Profile* and *Final Assessment Profile*, both of which contain assessment scales.

(b) Further Detail Prompt Material Sheets
Arranged to correspond with the recording profile pages as interleaved left-hand sheets in loose binders, these offer a further analysis of subfunctions and strategies within each teaching sub-area. By way of a modest form of pluralism, these further detail prompts were offered in four equivalent versions, also colour-coded: a *Prose* version, in which the sub-area is further articulated in the form of continuous, albeit terse prose; a *List* version, which simply reproduces the substantive items from the prose; a *Tree Diagram* version, in which the items are portrayed in a spatial hierarchy; and a *Concept Map* version, in which they are spatially presented within oval nodes (cf. Novak and Gowin, 1984; Tomlinson, 1995c), also allowing their embedded nature to be conveyed.

(c) Background and Guidelines For Use
Originally included as part of the mentor development course material, these embodied a number of the points made earlier in this chapter. The existence of alternative versions of the prompt material

Global level	Main areas	Sub-areas
Overall teaching competence	Explicit knowledge base	1. Subject knowledge and skills, curriculum resources
		2. Pupils and pedagogy
		3. Professional matters and commitment
	Planning and preparation	4. Clear learning goals appropriate for pupils, context, resources
		5. Adequate range of activities and resources for pupils, goals and resources
	Interactive teaching	6. Intelligent and effective assistance on pupil learning, organization and resourcing
		7. Effective assessment and monitoring of pupil learning activities and progress
		8. Appropriate relating to and influencing pupils, their behaviour, motivation and well-being
		9. Effective assessment and monitoring of pupil behaviour, motivation and well-being
	Wider professional roles	10. Wider educational role fulfilment through effective collaboration with various others
	Professional self-development	11. Development of explicit knowledge base of subject, pedagogy and professional matters
		12. Improvement of professional capabilities through appropriate mentoring, reflection and change

Figure 5.1   *An analysis of levels of competence in teaching
(NB three out of the four levels are shown here)*

was highlighted and users were invited to extend and amend this where they thought useful, particularly to cater for features specific to their subject area.

The importance of all levels of analysis in the profile was stressed, including the stance that overall judgement of teaching competence does not reduce to the mere aggregation of sub-area or main area ratings. Nevertheless, the profile record booklets do follow a 'bottom-up' order starting with sub-area (1) and leading to overall teaching competence at the end. Minimum assessment requirements were indicated as a way of ensuring thorough consideration of problematic cases. It was made clear that proficiency ratings are supposed to relate to what is expected of a newly qualified teacher teaching 'average pupils', with recognition that this may raise various types of problem, eg, 'needs attention' at the interim stage sounds more negative, when a 'developmental' approach might have allowed 'progressing well'.

(d) Lesson Observation Forms and Assessment Guidelines
The competence profile material was not intended for direct lesson observation, but rather for periodic review in the light of lesson obser-vation notes and other evidence from a student teaching and assessment file.

These materials and ideas were introduced gradually within our mentor training course, from a relatively early stage. It was not done by the core team who had designed and vetted the authoring of the course materials, but by subject-method tutors. This was for a variety of reasons, central amongst which were the need to engage our subject-method colleagues and to thereby respond to secondary teachers' and student-teachers' perceived identification with their subject areas.

THE INITIAL IMPACT OF COMPETENCE PROFILING IN SCHOOL-BASED ITE

Having offered this background of constructive critique and practical design, how do things actually seem to be turning out so far? We should certainly qualify what we have to say here with the reminder that 'so far' doesn't actually mean very much time and experience, given the scale of the changes in ITE, though this also means that we may be in a position to pick up trends which require response. What follows mainly concerns the secondary age-range and is based on our involvement in the LUSSP scheme just described, but also on the cur-rent piloting of our school-based primary Postgraduate Certificate in

Education (PGCE) and some access to the joint development of newly qualified teacher induction and mentoring schemes with neighbouring LEAs. In addition to this 'action research', we also attempted during the summer of 1994 to survey the competence profiling documentation which had been in use nationally across the 70 or so secondary PGCE courses during their first year of school-based arrangements; these data are still being analysed.[1] Our database is thus somewhat fragmented, if rich, so that the summary impressions we now present must also be somewhat tentative.

The national picture

Our survey managed to obtain relatively full competence profile documentation from just over 40 of the 70 *secondary* PGCE courses in England and Wales. The first impression was of the massive variation they showed in a number of features, but cluster analysis based on a relatively crude itemizing of competence aspects indicated two main groups each falling into two main sub-groups, the sub-group sizes being roughly equal. One of these sub-groups, about a quarter of our sample, was constituted by those HEI-school partnerships using the DfE competence formulation straight from circular 9/92, while the other sub-group of that main group used adapted versions of the DfE statements. The other main group represented attempts to plough a new furrow, including one sub-group involving explicit attempts to make their formulation serve the development of reflective teachers. By contrast, it is perhaps worth recording our impression at a recent Universities Council on the Education of Teachers workshop on competences in *primary* ITE that the great majority of the institutions present there were following the DfE formulation of circular 14/93. It should also be noted that about a fifth of the institutions responding to our survey pointed out firmly that they were in the process of revising their competence profile on the basis of the first year's experience.

Another general impression from the secondary phase documentation was that competence profiles seemed rarely to be functioning as the sole basis for adjudging students' success on the course and for NQT certification. Given that virtually none seemed to provide for any interrelating of the different levels of generality they did include (never more than three), this is perhaps a good thing. Both of these tendencies contribute to the impression that competence profiling is being deployed, but has not yet exactly 'swept the board' in the new ITE at secondary level, which may also be fortunate. Given the previous 'global professional assessment' approach, this is hardly surprising, but its significance is harder to evaluate.

Resistance to complex articulation?

Although we should point out the urgent need for systematic research into this area, we can say that the variation we noted regarding forms of profile and documentation did seem to be echoed in the responses to our LUSSP secondary profile and in the primary and NQT induction contexts to which we have had access. Thus there were some, a very few, who even initially welcomed and found interesting the articulation of teaching aspects we offered. Many found the profiles initially daunting, though in due course some of these seem to have come to value them and their detail. Others, more vociferous at least and probably a majority, seem to have taken against the notion of detailed articulation and these certainly included some of our colleagues, who were accused by one of our school-staff coordinators of having 'sabotaged' our efforts to present the new competence profiling approach intelligently. In a simple questionnaire evaluation exercise, an overwhelming majority of students responding expressed themselves dissatisfied with the competence documentation.

Persistence of traditional assumptions?

Of equal importance to the nature of these reactions are their possible causes. They were probably occasioned by a range of factors, from which one surely cannot discount traditional assumptions. A well-known 'paradox of skill' is that assisting the development of skill seems logically to require someone who is already proficient, but that such people conduct their action in very different and much more intuitive ways than do novices (Bereiter and Scardamalia, 1993; Gellatly, 1986; Tomlinson, 1995c). This would appear to be at work in the assumptions of some of our teacher and departmental colleagues that explicit detail of articulation is not needed in competence profiling. It may be even stronger than this, namely that there is still a folk psychology belief that when it comes to complex capabilities like teaching, one *either* talks about general principles and insights, *or* deals in details (cf. Tomlinson and Swift, 1992), when what one really needs is for both of these to be appropriately interrelated. Another relevant datum here is that our standing group of school representatives and university link tutors also opted for a simplifying revision of the competence profile prompt material for the second year.

Not a million miles from this (apparently, but this is an area which seems to have had surprisingly little investigation) was the student rejection of competence profile complexity. Similarly, some of our colleagues conducting a study of our students' beliefs about their acquisition of class management skill found that students expected to learn this skill mainly from immersion in action and talking to teachers, rather than from their university tutors, and certainly not from reading books!

Effects of under-resourcing and stress?

Quite apart from the effect of the traditional assumptions just considered, but pushing anyway in the same direction, must be the effects of the overwork and stress teachers have been under for a number of years and the lack of time for consultation with their colleagues. It seems clear that whatever the stances the new teacher-mentors bring to school-based ITE and however effective their preparation may or may not be, the quality of the whole enterprise is seriously threatened by resourcing levels. A number of school staff who had been involved with us previously in articled teacher schemes had commented in the run-up on the contrastingly low resourcing of the new school-based arrangements (Saunders *et al.*, 1995) and it is clear that whatever one thinks of the amounts of money passing from HEIs to schools in the new arrangements, the proportion finding its way into direct support of the new teacher preparation function varies enormously from school to school.

Given all this, it is hard not to be concerned that the cumulative effect in all too many cases may be that the teacher preparation function becomes a routinized and minimal affair. We never actually heard it amongst our teachers, but there was much, particularly amongst students, to remind one of the dictum that has been said to sum up too many UK surgeons' attitude towards the development of surgical skills: 'See one, do one, teach one'! The need we highlighted earlier, for the use of competence profiling and school-based teacher preparation generally to be informed by a well-grounded pedagogy, seems at least to be under some threat as things currently stand.

Quality assurance

We appear to be in a real dilemma as regards quality assurance and standards in ITE. Despite the above threats to their effective development, school-based partnerships probably offer, in principle, the best chance for assisting the development of intelligent teaching skill, since this does require reflective experiential immersion (Tomlinson, 1995c). But we thereby extend the teacher preparation function to a large number of teachers and their involvement as mentors with student-interns will give them by far the best basis for assessing these students for NQT certification. The task of quality assurance is thereby increased immeasurably. The potential role of external moderation seems both weak (given how little a moderator could sample compared to the breadth and closeness of school-based mentors), yet crucial.

The tension between assessment and development

Even if there were no difficulty in assuming communality of meaning and assessment using teaching profiles, there remain various forms of tension between their assessment and development functions. One is the perennial one between student and mentor, in which honest reflection can be threatened, at least on the surface, by the perceived need to succeed. Perhaps an even more serious threat to the potential of competence profiling is posed by the temptation which a common general version in particular would bring, namely that first appointments would be made on a count of the number of proficient competence aspects indicated or, even more crudely, through simplistic aggregation of any rating scales employed. The pressure on training providers to achieve in the league-tables of student employment could see an assessment inflation of unprecedented scale, further exacerbating the problem of quality assurance and comparability.

SOME SUGGESTIONS

The above concerns are, as we said, put forward tentatively, given the relatively informal and incomplete nature of the evidence. But their possible negative impact is such that they ought surely to be taken seriously. They ought of course to be given very thorough further discussion and analysis against systematic evidence, but our present scope limits us to making the following suggestions, which are designed to impinge on a number of the concerns referred to above:

- The TTA should *maintain a pluralism within consistency* regarding teaching competence formulations, whether for formative or summative use.

- In order to maximize the benefits of this approach and certainly insofar as it might consider the adoption of specific general models, it should *commission thorough research evaluation of the use of different forms of teaching profile*, including their validity and reliability and their effects, narrow and broader, short and longer term, under adequately sampled, realistic conditions. Such work should not be entrusted to any single team or methodology, but should be systematically triangulated at all levels.

- Similarly, steps should be taken to research thoroughly the actual amounts of time and quality of experience and assistance provided for student-teachers under school-based arrangements, including study of actual variations in deployment of existing resource levels and investigation of the benefits and costs of a wider range of resourcing, in particular resourcing that goes beyond current levels and approaches, for instance to that provided in articled teacher schemes.

- In order to combat the tensions between assessment and development functions of profiling suggested above, the TTA should commission research into ways in which ITE competence profiling may relate to further professional phases. As well as investigating the effects of separating or varying assessment and mentor-assistance roles within courses, this might include a possibility in which student-teacher profiles were *not* allowed to be used in deciding teaching appointments, though once appointed, the NQT would take their ITE profile into induction and further development, including appraisal.

NOTE

1. We should like to acknowledge the financial support for this work given by our own School of Education and by the Association of Teachers and Lecturers.

Chapter 6

Assessing Competence in Teacher Education

Rob Halsall

INTRODUCTION

Prior to 1992 an increasing number of teacher education courses – Postgraduate Certificate in Education (PGCE), Bachelor of Education (BEd) and Bachelor of Arts/Science with Qualified Teacher Status (BA/BSc with QTS) – had begun to approach more systematically the assessment of course outcomes in the context of a more searching examination of the functions of initial teacher education (ITE). In the main, these developments were based on profiling, the approaches to which varied along a continuum between two extremes. At one extreme was profiling as a mechanistic means of relating assessment to a set of prescribed competences. At the other extreme there were learner-centred strategies for helping students to take greater responsibility for, and reflect upon, their own progress.

Then in June 1992, the Department for Education issued Circular 9/92 (DfE, 1992) which, together with later guidance notes from the Council for the Accreditation of Teacher Education, advanced new criteria and procedures for secondary ITE. This established a framework within which student teachers are assessed against sets of competences relating to subject knowledge, subject application, classroom management, the assessment and recording of pupils' progress, and further professional development. A set of broadly similar criteria for primary ITE followed in November 1993, via Circular 14/93 (DfE, 1993a).

This 'official' impetus for competence-based teacher education (CBTE) was not unexpected given the wider debate about quality in education and training, the growing influence of the National Council for Vocational Qualifications (NCVQ) and critiques of ITE. To begin with, considerable suspicion and scepticism were aired concerning the use of competences in teacher education. In many cases this was due to a lack of understanding that there can be different definitions and models of competence. Most unease has centred around a narrow behaviourist approach. However, alternative or supplementary models do exist and where these have been considered it has been recognized that CBTE has many potential benefits. As Murphy *et al* (1993) have pointed out, it can:

● make explicit to both staff and students the skills, knowledge and understanding which have often been unstated and half-hidden

● help focus students' reflections on their own practice

● help staff to focus more systematically on whether opportunities are being provided to help students develop

● help clarify the relationship between subject application, education studies and school experience

● help clarify what elements of training are best delivered where

● improve the transition between ITE and the first years of teaching.

CBTE can also give practical expression to key professional values, knowledge, skills and processes; provide a framework for reviewing professional development, for assessment and for course construction and progression; and enhance partnership between schools and higher education institutions. Consequently,

> most people in teacher education do now recognise the value of using competences in some aspects of ITE... despite widespread unease about narrow behaviourist approaches to the specification and assessment of competences, an approach which recognises the importance of generic professional competences as well as specific classroom skills appears to be gaining support (Department of Education, Northern Ireland, 1993, pp. 2–3).

Certainly, there has been considerable debate concerning definitions and models of competence as they relate to professional courses (see, for example, other chapters in this book; Elliott, 1994; Gonczi, 1994; Whitty and Wilmott, 1991; Winter, 1992). It is not the intention here to review this debate though it will be drawn on later in this chapter. What I wish to focus on is one case study, originating pre-1992, and two particular issues it raises, especially in the context of circular 9/92 and in the light of a rapid shift towards competence approaches in education more generally. A fuller account of the case study is available in a report produced by the Didsbury School of Education (1993).

LEARNING CONTRACTS AND THE PGCE SECONDARY COURSE

The Didsbury School of Education, Manchester Metropolitan University: the beginnings of a competence-based approach

The context is a one-year PGCE secondary course which now has over 400 students. In 1991/2 the PGCE students, their tutors and associated schools became involved in the implementation of what we called the Professional Development Portfolio. This was to record student progress as a beginning teacher; achievements in understanding a range of educational issues; and areas for further exploration upon taking up a post. Its functions were to:

● provide a snapshot of progress through the course;

● assess levels of knowledge and standards of professional competence.

The portfolio comprised three sections:

● Learning contracts (which will later be dealt with at some length).

● Self-assessment of development as a teacher, based on reflections and evaluations written periodically during school experience as well as at the end of block teaching practices.

● Other elements of assessment, containing tutor- and teacher-written teaching practice reports (focused largely around professional competences) and tutor comment sheets in respect of assignments.

The key figure in guiding students through the process was the personal tutor (now, together with partnership school central mentors). Timetabled review sessions were incorporated into the course. These included individual tutorials, group sessions, and peer group reviews.

Nine topics were identified that would be subject to learning contracts. The wide range of these is partly accounted for by the fact that the course is based overwhelmingly around subject applications; there is no separate education studies component. The contracts were – and are – in the areas of:

● personal and social education and the pastoral role

● equal opportunities

● special educational needs

● the able and gifted child

- health education and safety
- links with parents and the wider community
- economic understanding and industrial awareness
- information technology
- the contractual, legal and administrative responsibilities of teachers.

Each area has sets of prescribed knowledge/skills and application/ experience components. Students must show evidence of competence in all of these. They can also offer evidence of *additional* work/experience/ knowledge in the areas, and are expected to then identify elements which are in need of extension work. Space does not permit an account of all nine areas. Personal and Social Education is presented as an example. The prescribed knowledge and skills are:

a. Knowledge of what constitutes the pastoral role of the tutor.

b. Awareness of PSE in the hidden and overt curriculum.

c. Awareness of issues surrounding confidentiality and ethics.

The prescribed application and experience are:

i. Experienced the role of pastoral tutor on teaching practice.

ii. Provided examples of active tutorial techniques in school or in college.

Document 6.1 represents these and indicates the requirements that students must meet in providing evidence of their achievements. It also gives, in section C, the opportunity for describing additional outcomes and for identifying extension areas (section D). Document 6.2 comprises the student guidelines which include illustrative sources of evidence, examples of issues for students to bear in mind and suggestions for background reading.

How might Circular 9/92 affect what we have been doing? It has not had any significant effect on how we conceptualize CBTE. It has, however, stimulated a speedier response to extending our approach to other elements of the course and, of course, because of Circular 14/93, to other programmes, most notably the Primary PGCE and the BEd. Work is still ongoing here. However, in our further development I hope we will continue to be mindful of two particular issues that have been raised in the context of the competence debate generally. They are issues to which we have given much thought in our developments so far.

Document 6.1   *PGCE Secondary Course. Professional Development Portfolio*

Title	Student

PERSONAL AND SOCIAL EDUCATION AND THE PASTORAL ROLE		
A. Knowledge/skills	**Evidence**	**Signature**
1. Knowledge of what constitutes the pastoral role of the tutor		
2. Aware of personal and social education in the hidden and overt curriculum		
3. Aware of issues surrounding confidentiality and ethics		

B. Application/ experience	Evidence	Signature
1. Experienced the role of tutor during teaching practice		
2. Provided examples of active tutorial techniques in school or college		
C. Additional work, experience, knowledge		
D. Areas for extension		
Student signature	**Personal tutor signature**	

Document 6.2   *PGCE Secondary Course. Professional Development Portfolio. Guidelines to students – Personal and Social Education and the Pastoral Role*

The recommended texts in these guidelines are available from the library on the Didsbury site ... (*details of resources removed by editors*).

Part A. Knowledge/skills

1. Knowledge of what constitutes the pastoral role of the tutor.

Examples of sources of evidence:

- Main subject sessions.

- School experience, for example,
    * observation during early school visits
    * observation at teaching practice school (see observation checklist)
    * teaching practice file (should contain background details of school pastoral system and policies, including guidance notes to staff)
    * teaching practice (notes/observations of shadowing/experiencing tutor role).

- Assignments, for example, the school day assignment criteria referring to the diverse activities which make up the school day.

Background reading (*details of resources removed by editors*).

2. Awareness of Personal and Social Education (PSE) in the hidden and overt curriculum.

Examples of sources of evidence:

- Main subject sessions

- Teaching experience of PSE as a timetabled subject or in active tutorial sessions

- Experience of PSE in the hidden curriculum (for example, through the school ethos, extra-curricular activities, other aspects of the school day)

- Assignments (where appropriate to criteria)

- Observation in teaching practice school

Examples of questions you may wish to ask:

- How is PSE timetabled – during tutorial or timetabled subject time?

- Who teaches it – class tutor or PSE team?

- Have teachers had initial or in-service training in PSE?

- What 'content' and which 'skills' comprise the PSE syllabus?

- Is PSE permeated through the curriculum?

- What status does PSE have amongst teachers and pupils?

- Is there a conflict between PSE objectives and the ethos of the school – do they influence each other?
- Are you able to contribute to the PSE programme through your main subject or interests?

Background reading (*details of resources removed by editors*).

3. Awareness of issues surrounding confidentiality and ethics.

Examples of sources of evidence:

- Main subject sessions
- School observation/experience, for example details of the school pastoral system, including guidance to teachers.

Background reading (*details of resources removed by editors*).

Part B. Application/experience

Experience the role of the tutor on teaching practice.

It is important that you experience the role of tutor on at least one of your teaching practices. You may find it helpful to shadow, observe or team with a tutor on first teaching practice and take the full tutoring role on the second practice. You should negotiate with the teacher in charge of students during observation week in your placement school.

Evidence for this may take many forms, for example:

- School teaching practice report
- Tutor teaching practice report
- Student teaching practice self-evaluation report
- Teaching practice file containing comment on and evaluation of tutor role
- Assignments, where relevant to criteria

2. Provided evidence of active tutorial techniques in school or in college.

Examples of sources of evidence:

- Main subject sessions
- Teaching practice or college file containing lesson plans and evaluations of active tutorial work
- Materials generated in college

Useful classroom materials include: (*details of resources removed by editors*).

You may wish to extend your experience or the range of applications by choosing to take the third term PSE option.

LEARNER AUTONOMY

One of the main reasons we introduced learning contracts was to use negotiated, formative assessment and its concomitant demands for professional deliberation to develop the skills of autonomous learning. There are various views as to what these skills constitute, but there exists some consensus that they include:

- diagnosing one's own learning needs

- formulating one's own learning objectives

- identifying for oneself necessary resources to achieve these

- taking the initiative in the use of these

- assessing one's progress and achievements

- identifying and providing evidence as to these.

These skills embrace the notions of review, reflection, target-setting and action planning. Does our approach with learning contracts match up to this? I feel that it does, to a certain extent. Students themselves identify particular elements of the contract they wish to target at any point in time. It is not expected that students will address elements within or across contracts in the same sequence as each other. It is not assumed that they all have the same learning needs either at the beginning of the course or at any point during it. Considerable responsibility rests with students to arrange for the meeting of their needs:

> the initiative lies with you to negotiate opportunities to fulfil particular items ... at specified times during the year you will be in a position to ... decide when and how you are going to try and meet these targets (PGCE Handbook).

Students also have an active role in self-assessment and in the provision of evidence of their achievements. A number of review sessions are built into the course. Students are expected to arrive at these having reflected on, and recorded, progress and having gathered evidence of that progress. They will have discussed some aspects of this with school staff and peers, but at the student-tutor review sessions there will be discussion on the entirety, out of which will emerge targets for further development. Here, section D of the learning contract form will be significant, particularly at the end of the course and it will, we hope, be used profitably by the student and relevant staff in his or her first appointment.

Out of the list of learner autonomy skills I have yet to refer to the formulation of one's own objectives. Clearly, our learning contracts – both those in use now and others being developed – contain prescribed outcomes or objectives. Section C does allow for additional work, experience and knowledge to be recorded. However, these might not have been planned for by students but, rather, be *post hoc* in nature. In this approach, there is no necessary requirement that students do engage in a process of formulating their own objectives related to any additional work that they do. Certainly, in the wealth of guidance materials on contracts there is no explicit orientation to that. My own view is that this constitutes a significant gap in our desire to encourage the development of autonomous learners, and is one which needs to be narrowed in future. The fuller implementation of the 9/92 competences must be undertaken with this in mind.

REDUCTIVISM

The competence movement generally can be seen as atomistic, deconstructing activities into allegedly constituent skills via a process of functional analysis which breaks activities down until they are usable as 'standards'. Such an approach might be appropriate in some areas of occupational activity, but is it in relation to teaching? Several writers have argued that a reductionist emphasis can be damaging to the quality of the overall learning process. To Jones and Moore (1993) it can 'produce impoverished and simplistic accounts of complex social interactions. By decontextualising skills ... these reductive procedures construct partial, disembedded representations of the complex social interactions of work' (p. 388).

The result can be a curriculum which focuses upon narrow technical competency. Here too, then, we must be careful in implementing 9/92, though it is probably fair to say that the circular has taken a broadly-based approach to competences and, *if* handled professionally, reductivism can be avoided. As Furlong (1992) points out:

> In each area ... the Circular is open to narrow as well as broad interpretations. A narrowly mechanistic approach to initial teacher education is not demanded by the Circular. If that is the result it will be because we have imposed it on ourselves (pp. 5–6).

Certainly, we are mindful of this issue. ITE courses do have much in common with NCVQ competence-based programmes: there is considerable on-the-job training and many competences are assessable by direct observation of performance. However, in relation to the 'job' of teaching, it needs to be recognized that workplace skills are applied within specific contexts which vary according to circumstances; that there are competences that are not conducive to assessment by observation alone, not least those relating to underpinning knowledge and understanding; and that teaching is more than the sum of a collection of discrete competences. Equally important is the fact that any competence framework for ITE cannot and must not exclude such dimensions as consideration of the values and roles of practitioners, the goals and ethos of the institutions in which they operate or the ability to raise questions about the wider socio-political context and, indeed, about the very set of competences which dominate one's course. To quote from the introduction to our own policy for the preparation of teachers:

> Competences are related to a view of knowledge and professional practice. Each is grounded in a range of values which are by their nature pluralistic or controversial. It is within this overarching concept of the process of professional development that competences are acquired, extended and used at a variety of levels ... they will be used in ways that cannot be predetermined. They will be used in different educational circumstances and within a wider educational perspective than a simple use of common sense or consensual application. In particular, their use in crude checklists is rejected. ...
> Our understanding of the effective teacher is that of a professional communicator who can make decisions and solve problems, who can manage and not just survive change, and who can be a significant influence in a democratic and ethical society. Such a view rejects any suggestion that a teacher is a mere educational technocrat without wider responsibilities (Didsbury School of Education, 1993).

Fundamental to effective teaching, we believe, is the development of:

● Breadth and depth of knowledge and skills.

● A range of professional values relating to, for example, the promotion of equal opportunities and recognition of the need to respect the beliefs and values of others.

● Self-awareness which, among other things, involves taking account of a variety of situations and circumstances in which the skills of teaching will be used.

In short, skills cannot be de-contextualized and the concept of the ethical and reflective practitioner needs to be central to the development of the effective teacher.

WAYS FORWARD

In order to address these points, a model of CBTE must be developed which is more than a list of specific tasks. Some useful work has started here, not least in the deliberations of the working group on competences as part of the review of ITE in Northern Ireland:

> we began to see that a simple list of competences ... could not convey the totality of what we wanted to say about the professional competence of a teacher ... the atomisation of professional knowledge, judgement and skill into discrete competences inevitably fails to capture the essence of professional competence (Department of Education, Northern Ireland, 1993, p. 4).

Their way forward has been to identify competences relating to knowledge (for example, knowledge of children, learning, subject, curriculum, teacher's role) and professional skills (for example, skill in classroom methodology, class management, assessment and recording), and to identify the underlying qualities of the teacher which enable him or her to pull the individual competences together and apply them. These qualities relate to professional values, professional and personal development, communication and relationships, and synthesis and application.

In similar vein has been the 'alternative' competence format devised by the ASSET programme in social work at Anglia Polytechnic University (see Chapter 4, this volume). Here, the decision was to specify core assessment criteria which bring together individual competences. These comprise commitment to professional values, continuous professional learning, affective awareness, effective communication, executive effectiveness, synthesis of knowledge and intellectual flexibility; as Winter (1992, p. 114) puts it: 'educational criteria derived from an elaborated theory of the reflective professional practitioner'. In these ways the contextualization of skills, the issue of values, and the reflective imperative are being taken on board.

At Didsbury, debate concerning the most appropriate way forward is well under way in relation to both secondary and primary provision. Here I will focus, for illustrative purposes, on the latter, where progress is captured in an internal document, 'Seeds of a Way Forward: towards a possible structure of competences'. The competences that we are developing will be predicated upon our view of the effective teacher as discussed above. The approach to be adopted consists of identifying key categories and major perspectives.

The categories embody professional attitudes, knowledge, skills and practice. They comprise knowledge and understanding of:

a. Children's learning – goals and expectations, process and implementation, analysis.

b. The role of the teacher – classroom roles and implementation, wider professional activities.

c. The curriculum – the whole curriculum, teaching subjects and their uses, cross curricular activities.

d. Professional skills and their implementation – planning for teaching and learning, classroom management and methodology, evaluation/assessment/recording.

e. The principles and means of furthering personal professional development – review of progress, self-appraisal, identification of priorities for personal, future development.

The perspectives are:

a. Technical, relating to the knowledge of the mechanics of teaching, learning, planning, managing, implementing, resourcing and evaluating or assessing all aspects of a teacher's work.

b. Contextual, relating to an understanding of the school and classroom context in which the work of a teacher takes place and which includes the student's personal standpoint and intentions.

c. Interpretive, relating to the wider social and ethical perspectives within which the teacher works and to the kind of teacher the student seeks to become.

Within each category there will be individual competence items including, but not solely comprising, those in circular 14/93. These will provide indicative evidence of achievement. It is an assumption of this scheme that all categories and individual items are capable of being understood in terms of each perspective and that each perspective necessarily informs all practice. Competences are related to progression throughout the course with periodic, holistic review. The vehicle for this might well be a journal, the contents of which would be evidence of professional development and include elements of work that contribute to degree classification. At each point of assessment, which might be, for example, in term 1, 2 and 3 or year 1, 2, 3 and 4, there could be stage descriptions representing an account of what learners might be expected to have achieved by that stage in the course progression. These would include the Circular 14/93 competences as captured within our categories but would also be based on the three perspectives. The categories would apply at each stage of assessment but the detail under each perspective would differ according to the stage. However, each perspective would be related to each item under the categories.

We still have a long way to go but there is a clear sense of direction which has been informed by earlier efforts within the PGCE Secondary course and by current debate concerning the limitations of a narrowly behaviourist model of competences for professional courses.

Acknowledgements

It would have been impossible to have written this chapter without the developmental and evaluative work undertaken by many of my colleagues at the Didsbury School of Education. Particular mention must be made of Jack Hogbin, Dave Hustler and Janet Palmer.

Chapter 7

Recording Achievement in Higher Education

David Hustler

INTRODUCTION

Records of Achievement and the Recording of Achievement, jointly referred to as RoA in this chapter, seem to have caught the imagination of many staff within higher education over the last few years (Assiter and Shaw, 1993). Although vocabularies vary, with 'profiles' and 'profiling' often being the favoured wording in higher education, we are finding the same enthusiastic RoA cultures developing as those which were prominent within the Technical and Vocational Education Initiative (TVEI) in secondary schools and colleges during the 1980s (Barnes, 1989; Entwistle, 1992). We could certainly go further back to the work of Barbara Pearce associated with profiling (Pearce, 1982; 1983). Of key relevance for this book, of course, is that some approaches to the assessment of competences, within a large variety of emerging higher education schemes, assign a central place to RoA, though we should note from the outset that for some this association is anathema!

Unlike many of the other chapters in the book, this chapter is not concerned with the details of or the rationale behind a particular approach to the assessment of competences, to the use of learning contracts or with RoA schemes within a higher education institution (HEI). The initial question here is just why RoA have become matters of interest and development for such institutions? In attempting to answer this question, I would argue that we learn something about the current changing nature of our higher education system and the differing initiatives which are driving those changes as perceived by those working within that system. In this way we are addressing central issues to do with the institutional contexts within which moves towards both RoA and at times the assessment of competences are taking place. As will be seen, however, that initial question also raises some concerns about the variety of agendas leading to an interest in RoA, both within and across universities.

The substantive materials for this chapter come from an external evaluation of the Recording Achievement and Higher Education Project. This project, based in the North-West and North of England, involved staff in 15 universities and colleges of higher education and 11 local education authorities, together with associated schools and colleges. Formally funded by the Employment Department and by the participant institutions, the project ran between September 1991 and August 1993, and was extremely ambitious both in its size and number of collaborating institutions and in its initial aims. These aims were:

1. 'To encourage ... HEIs to develop their admissions processes through the increased use of RoA as important sources of evidence'.

2. 'To encourage HEIs to use recording achievement as a formative process to improve the quality and effectiveness of learning'.

3. 'To improve the progression of students' learning experiences between schools, colleges and HEIs through the use of Recording Achievement'.

4. 'To promote to education providers and to young people and their parents Recording Achievement as being relevant to all levels of ability'.

The full report of this project and its evaluation is available and has been disseminated through the Universities' and Colleges' Admissions Service and the Employment Department (Greenwood and Hustler, 1994). In the following section the focus is solely on the perceptions and viewpoints of a wide range of higher education staff associated with the project. A puzzle for the evaluation team was just why the degree of involvement from staff in higher education was as extensive, continuing and increasingly enthusiastic. At least, this seemed to be the case from an extensive interviewing and re-interviewing process over the life of the project. These staff included: course tutors and course leaders, admissions tutors, deans and vice-chancellors, heads of departments, staff associated with particular projects such as the Enterprise in Higher Education (EHE) initiative, personal tutors and staff working in areas such as student services.

In what follows, illustrative extracts from the interview materials are loosely associated with typical differing emphases which seemed to be informing participants' interest in RoA involvement. It seemed important to present sufficient quotations for the reader to develop a sense of the materials and the appropriateness or otherwise of the attempt to classify them in relation to differing motivations. A question for the reader of this chapter concerns the ways in which, if at all, some of these extracts and imputed motivations connect with their own interest in RoA and, more particularly, with their views as to how RoA may or may not connect with the assessment of competences. In the final section there is a discussion of some of the implications of these materials for understanding developments in higher education and for clarifying our own approaches in the area of RoA and competences. In this final discussion I will also touch on debates which have taken place within a research seminar group, funded by the ESRC, to consider competences and teacher education. There are some interesting parallels.

Before moving to the next section, it should be noted that the emphasis here is not on the virtues or vices of RoA, whether as product or as a process. It is assumed that the reader has some familiarity with the notion of RoA on which there is now a developing and accessible literature (Assiter and Shaw, 1993; Broadfoot, 1990; Fenwick *et al.*, 1992). What was it then about RoA that attracted the project participants from higher education?

THE INTEREST IN ROA

The process of learning in HE – the student at the centre

The RoA then isn't used as a transfer document but as part of a process encouraging more reflective students who are able to assess achievements and action plan skills recognized as significant for HE development within courses.

The gradual development of a philosophy of negotiation and target-setting centred on the student may well be enhanced by work undertaken in the Enterprise area, thus being given a higher profile within the institution.

It's the process which is crucial to learning: students reflecting on their progress and formulating new directions... the recording achievement process is all about learning.

Several respondents seemed to place at the centre an interest in the relationship between recording achievement and certain learning processes. Vocabularies differed (active learning; student-centred learning; action learning; etc.) but from many came comments reminiscent of evaluation reports in the early days of TVEI concerning active learning and experiential learning, and more recently some versions of flexible learning. In short, some participants were drawn to the project because it either opened up new ways of thinking about the nature of the student learning experience, or connected with existing commitments to certain forms of learning. Levels of sophistication varied: for some we would characterize the involvement as akin to conversion, for others it supported long-standing efforts to stress certain approaches to learning. For some, the project provided frameworks for thinking anew about the student learning experience in a context where their institution was prioritizing this. On occasion, there was explicit reference to the notion of student 'empowerment' and this will be returned to in the final discussion.

Appropriate learning within HE – the student as a whole person and generic skills

There should be much more recording of achievement and not just academic achievement... better exemplification of what students have done in their time in HE should be there for all to see.

Companies offering industrial placements give an indication of key attributes they are looking for – many of which are non-academic. RoAs were found to be particularly useful in matching up company criteria with the abilities of applicants.

An RoA is useful from the point of view of its process, in relation to the development of target-setting and action planning within HE. It also has value in gauging performance in respect of generic or core skills revealing more about the 'whole person' rather than just their academic achievements.

We move here to concerns, long associated with recording achievement, about the relevance within HE of attributes, skills and experiences, which are 'more than just academic'. For some respondents the interest connects with attempts in particular courses to integrate work-based and 'academic' learning, often in relation to models of core skills. Here there are close connections with many of the developments directly or indirectly stimulated by the Employment Department such as the EHE initiative. More generally, some respondents were revisiting and reformulating the essential nature of the higher education learning experience.

Learning outcomes and competences: knowing what the student has acquired

A well-designed process for recording achievement ... if designed and implemented properly... would lead to all of our students being very critically aware of what they are supposed to be getting out of our courses, what they are actually getting, where it is taking them and what else they need to do to build on what they have already learnt.

It's about being explicit about the outcomes of learning and the competences acquired by students.

We do need to be much clearer than we have been about what students have actually learnt within the institution: some form of record of that achievement is one way forward in this area.

The debate surrounding competences and learning outcomes – their purposes, shades of meaning, how best to harmonize them – is not resolved as yet, certainly in terms of the tensions between developmental and summative assessment functions. Respondents saw RoA as promoting explicitness about learning outcomes, but in explaining why this was viewed as a virtue, they reflected the continuing arguments surrounding this area, many of which are raised elsewhere in this book. The rest of the extracts in this section can be associated with differing arguments concerning the benefits of and need for that explicitness: there is, of course, a parallel with many of the arguments driving the competency debate.

Quality audits and accountability: the students and others as customers

The link here (in relation to quality audit work) with RoA is being explicit, perhaps in contractual terms, about what an institution will provide and the responsibilities on students and on the institution.

The discussion group identified the growing relevance of RoA within HE, to help staff deal with personal tutoring, in an age of mass HE and as 'evidence' in relation to quality audit and assessment, which looked for standards and sound practices in relation to 'the totality of the student learning experience' and in relation to student charters, which set certain requirements for customer care.

Procedures on the student support side will be checked by bodies such as the Academic Audit. It's useful therefore to get involved from a mercenary point of view.

Employers have a right to know what potential employees have learned during their time with us... and the public has a right to know more generally what their money has been spent on.

The assessment of course design and teaching/learning standards has become an important item on the higher education agenda, as has the auditing of systems for ensuring the quality of provision. At the time of our evaluation it was not yet clear what the criteria would be in relation to funding. It might be useful to note, however, that the Quality in Higher Education Project – based at the University of Central England – identified over 100 criteria as indicators of quality in higher education. Only ten achieved substantial consensus and amongst these were the following, which some respondents drew on in relation to their interest in RoA: students receive useful feedback from assessment and are kept informed of progress; students are encouraged to be actively involved in, and given responsibility for, learning; students leave with transferable knowledge and skills.

Increasing student numbers and diminishing resources – the students will have to take more responsibility

Anything which reduces the student number workload will be received like manna.

Students will have to take more responsibility for their own learning, given the numbers involved ... and we need to find ways which will help them do this.

The position adopted here seemed to involve the view that RoA and associated notions of flexible learning could provide a way forward in response to the sheer pressure of numbers. The interest here seems to be not so much linked with a sense that students *should* take responsibility for their own learning, but more that students *would have to* take more responsibility, given current pressures on universities. RoA is seen as one possible solution to an institutional problem.

Modularity and credit transfer – student pathways

We would identify the role of RoA in HE as assisting in the process of mapping out learning paths and in providing a place to keep 'credits'. RoA in this context is seen primarily as a vehicle to track learning and plan pathways, through new modular course structures.

The move towards modular courses was recognized as creating a need for more student/tutor reviewing, concerning subject/course choices. The role of discussion/negotiation underpinned by reference to appropriate documentation, eg, RoA, was seen as vital to the success of student learning and student choice.

As students move into and out of HE and across different sections within the university, we have to have material and systems through which we can match students to courses and take good account of their previous achievements.

The question of phased entry and accelerated degrees and differential output points, connects completely with the importance of understanding what someone actually did ... increasing numbers and pressures mean we will have to ... find ways of motivating students to learn how to learn, for their degree and for their lifelong learning. This involves placing more responsibility upon the student ... and differing responsibilities upon the institution. The RoA here is a device *for* making challenges explicit and tracking how you resolve them ... this is also a device for avoiding replicating old learning experiences.

These comments spell out in more detail perceived relationships between RoA and institutional moves in the areas of modularity and credit transfer. The emphases vary somewhat but we find here an even closer link with many of the arguments behind competency developments and more especially the assessment of competences. The final extract above leads us into a final set of arguments: those associated with changing notions of access, boundaries between higher education and other institutions and the very nature of university 'missions'.

Widening access, a diversifying student body, and differing relationships between HE and feeder institutions – the mission at the centre

We have an admissions policy based on giving entry to those who will most benefit. RoA may help us decide who to admit.

The advent of GNVQ could be another route of persuasion (to take RoA on board). Staff do seem interested in the qualification.

Contact with pre- and post-18 institutions through the project has provided insights into practices which others are developing and using. Perceptions about RoA have developed further through local liaison work with schools and colleges. It is a shared understanding of the value of the process which has been most potent in pulling people together from different sectors.

RoA does seem to speak, in a variety of ways, to what we feel our purpose as a university is – our mission statement captures this. It also brings us into meaningful discussions with the institutions working with students before we do, certainly within the region. The RoA project and other associated projects link, in my view, with our commitment to mass higher education and to a changing notion of the typical university student.

DISCUSSION

We have not associated the extracts above with our interviewees' institutional positions within HEIs, but it is interesting to remember, as noted earlier, that they do stem from a large variety of institutional roles. Clearly, for some respondents the interest is, naturally enough, associated with a very particular current involvement or institutional role. A course leader grappling with modularization could see RoA processes as important for programme coherence; a group of tutors involved in a course with extensive placement elements might see RoA as providing a possible solution to tracking, documenting or assessing student experience; an admissions tutor could see the potential relevance of RoA within admissions; others might see potential links between RoA and a variety of elements associated with the university mission; others would stress the relationships between RoA and developing GNVQ work. A tutor concerned with projects such as Enterprise in Higher Education could see associations between RoA and an emphasis on experiential learning or profiling.

We would argue more generally that the spread and range of interest is indicative of how certain interconnected broad movements, initiatives and pressures, associated with HE currently, are having some impact on the experience of an increasing number of HE personnel. These would include:

- increasing and widening participation, together with the emerging debate on non-traditional entry routes and NCVQ developments;
- the quality assessment agenda; the employer perspective and the 'world of work';
- the developing focus on the student learning experience and the nature of learning outcomes;
- the diminution of resources, student numbers and the need to find ways of students taking more responsibility for their own learning;
- the lifelong learning agenda;
- the moves to modularity;

- the vocabularies of student empowerment, student choice, as well as consumerism and the charter movement;

- the revising of university missions and the juggling for university identity and relative position;

- the loosening of boundaries between higher education and post-16 institutions;

- the changing views concerning what might count as an appropriate higher education learning environment;

- the interest in obtaining funding relating to teaching and learning within higher education.

One feature of these materials then is that they show how major changes and developments within the higher education sector are leading staff to see RoA as a fruitful way forward. At the same time, however, it is absolutely crucial to take note of the different agenda which are operating here: the different ways in which RoA are seen as relevant by different stakeholders within higher education institutions.

It might be argued that the language of RoA was a flexible vehicle for associating respondents' own immediate priorities and institutional roles with the developing priorities of senior management. We could also add another speculation concerning the mix of what might be viewed as pragmatic and principled motives informing participation in the project. For many respondents, RoA seemed to hold out the prospect of finding solutions to current pressures, imperatives and problems, in a way which one could be happy about in a principled sense. Student learning, said one, 'should be our focus and students should become more autonomous and responsible for their own learning': this might sit comfortably in relation to 'our need to solve student numbers pressures and respond to quality audits'; 'we do need to adapt our assessment and support system to take account of a changing student body' said another, 'RoA can help us here in taking fuller account of the broader student experience and what students bring with them'. It will have been noted that the classification of interview extracts in the final section above moved progressively from 'the student at the centre' to 'the mission at the centre'.

There are some powerful parallels between the varying perceptions of the relevance of RoA and the different positions protagonists take regarding competences and more particularly the assessment of competences. These differences were apparent within the membership of an ESRC research seminar group looking at competences and teacher education. Several of the members of this group, including Richard

Winter, Michael Eraut, John Elliott and Rob Moore have been referred to in earlier chapters in this book and there is no need to outline their positions anew. At the most general level, however, disputes centre around whether approaches to the assessment of competences are empowering for students, through, amongst other features, the demystification of assessment procedures, or whether such approaches entrap students in a narrow, decontextualized and mechanistic entry to professions so that they in fact become deskilled and deprofessionalized. Even when we move away from the Department for Education position on competences (see Chapter 7, this volume) to the much more developed thinking associated with the Employment Department (see Chapter 3, this volume), the argument continues as to whether this or that approach to the assessment of competences can or cannot perform the developmental purposes claimed for it as far as students are concerned.

RoA, especially when the concern is with the processes of recording achievement associated with reviewing and previewing, are commonly viewed as developmental and empowering for students. This is part of an emerging higher education culture, as it was earlier within TVEI for schools and colleges. Whether the vocabulary is one of RoA or profiling or learning contracts, these are at the friendly end of current approaches to recording and student assessment within higher education. There are now emerging a number of sets of case studies concerning the use of RoA within higher education. As in the book by Assiter and Shaw (1993), some issues and tensions are commonly pointed to in the editorial chapters: tensions to do with the relationship between RoA and assessment, with what some would see as the over-individualized emphasis built into RoA, with intrusion into students' lives via RoA, with matters concerning ownership of and final control over RoA. However, although these tensions are discussed in such texts, such discussion seems to be buried in the wealth of case studies describing particular schemes and possible ways forward.

The differences of viewpoint within the same institution regarding the relevance of RoA become especially crucial when it comes to course development and implementation and the difficulties are most apparent where RoA enter into a close relationship with institutional approaches to assessment. Many particular versions of the implementation of RoA within higher education do seem to be intended to serve a variety of, at times, conflicting needs. They relate to different parts of the classification presented in the last section. It is the students who are at the hard end of these schemes.

It is not being suggested here that any particular approach to RoA in an assessment context relating to a competency framework can *not* serve different needs and interests. It is, however, being strongly argued that any such scheme must be closely inspected for the ways in which it relates to differing agendas and the question must be posed as to whether it can serve those different needs. Secondary schools and colleges learnt some hard lessons here and not just about resourcing issues. One major issue concerned the prevalence of a considerable gap between enthusiastic staff positions on the virtues of RoA and the perceptions of their students. One feature of student disenchantment for some involves a growing awareness on their part that RoA, while sold to them initially in terms of 'the learner at the centre', were, in fact, very much designed primarily to meet institutional needs. Given the extent to which the language of student empowerment, in a variety of senses, pervades discussion of RoA, it must be crucial for us to at least avoid the ironic position where we disempower our students through our own lack of clarity and their potential confusion regarding RoA and the assessment of competences.

Chapter 8

Assessing Competence in Engineering Project Management

Richard Carter and Bob Neal

INTRODUCTION

The course which is the subject of this chapter is an industrially-based MSc in Engineering Project Management. The course began in 1985 as a joint venture between the Engineering Department of Lancaster University and the Training Department of Smiths Industries Aerospace and Defence Ltd (Carter and Cooke, 1987). The aim of the course was to give experienced, high-flying, engineers the skills needed to manage project teams. From the outset it was recognized that this aim implied the development, and hence the assessment, of competence. Our understanding of what constitutes competence in engineering project management has grown over the period of nearly ten years since the course began. During this time over a hundred students have undertaken real and sometimes major projects in industries as diverse as pharmaceuticals, offshore oil, electronics, automotive and food production. Their experiences have provided a laboratory in which the course tutors could discover what are the essential features of competence in project management and how these may be assessed in a working environment. We have come to recognize that competence involves more than merely a collection of individual skills, necessary as those are. In the demanding world of engineering the competent manager must be able to exercise a wide range of skills in relationship to one another. Thus, in our view, competence is a *metaskill* (Burgoyne and Stuart, 1976) which subsumes the collection of individual skills.

Although the course is directed primarily at the development of competence, it also leads to a postgraduate degree. Our understanding of this aspect has also grown through our experience. We consider it important that our students should be aware of the context of human knowledge relevant to their professional work. They should be able to draw on that knowledge to illuminate their experiences and to provide a

123

basis for personal development. The academic range of the course is wide, as will be seen from the description of its content below. The emphasis in teaching is therefore upon awareness of the key concepts and methods in a range of disciplines. The students are expected to be responsible for their own learning and to build on what they have learnt through private study. The function of the tutors is to facilitate learning rather than dispense received wisdom *ex cathedra*. For this reason, most of the teaching is through workshops rather than formal lectures. Special attention is paid to the development of students' learning and problem-solving skills at the start of the course.

From our experience we have concluded that there are a number of features which are essential in competence-based education:

- the objectives of the course must be clear, comprehensive, measurable and communicated to the students

- the structure and delivery of the course must be consonant with the objectives

- the assessment of the students' work must be carried out with reference to the objectives against known criteria. There must be no hidden curriculum.

In the sections which follow we discuss the ways in which these features have been realized in our course.

OBJECTIVES

The objectives of education are commonly specified as desired outcomes in terms of knowledge, skills and personal qualities. Table 8.1 shows the summary of a taxonomy of educational objectives incorporating these three levels (Carter, 1985). In a competence-based course such as this, the focus of attention is naturally on the particular skills required to achieve competence. It is true that there is also an essential knowledge base, but this supports the skills rather than being an end in its own right. In our experience the development of competence is closely linked to personal development at the third level (shown as the top row of Table 8.1) of the taxonomy. We have certainly observed in our students the growth of openness to new ideas and to the value of people, for example. But we have not yet attempted to include personal qualities in the statement of the course objectives.

Initially the objectives for the course were expressed in terms of competence in certain skills together with awareness of the skills of

Table 8.1   *A taxonomy of objectives for professional education*

Mental characteristics	Attitudes and values	Personality characteristics	Spiritual qualities
Openness	Things	Integrity	Appreciation
Agility	Self	Initiative	Response
Imagination	People	Industry	
Creativity	Groups	Emotional	
	Ideas	resilience	
Mental skills	**Information skills**	**Action skills**	**Social skills**
Organization	Acquisition	Manual	Cooperation
Analysis	Recording	Organizing	Leadership
Evaluation	Remembering	Decision making	Negotiation and
Synthesis	Communication	Problem solving	persuasion
			Interviewing
Factual knowledge		**Experiential knowledge**	
Facts		Experience	
Structures		Internalization	
Procedures		Generalization	
Concepts		Abstraction	
Principles			

experts in other disciplines with whom the students would have to work. It was soon discovered that this approach was too prescriptive. There might not be opportunities in any given main project for demonstrating all the skills listed. At the same time other skills, which had not been listed, could be needed in order to manage the project effectively. The course objectives were therefore revised as a shorter list of generalized skills from the second level of Table 8.1 based on the main activities required for problem-solving (Koberg and Bagnall, 1981). The current statement of objectives is:

By the end of the course a successful student will have demonstrated the ability to act as an effective project leader in an industrial context and, specifically, the ability to:

● Define tasks

● Generate ideas

- Make and justify decisions
- Plan and control activities
- Evaluate the results of activities
- Communicate effectively
- Work effectively with people
- Continue personal development.

Each of these abilities is further defined by examples of the ways in which it might be demonstrated. For example:

> **Evaluate the results of activities** by testing a product or system, by reviewing progress and achievement and revising plans and objectives, by reviewing personal lessons learnt from experience, by reviewing the success of a project against commercial objectives.

An individual is unlikely to be able to provide evidence of competence to match all of the examples given but every student should be able to show competence in the generic skill in some way. This set of objectives has been in use, unchanged, for about eight years. It is included in the course brochure, reiterated to the students at the start of the course and is the basis of all assessment. The forms and other documents used by the assessors are issued to these MSc students so that they understand as clearly as possible what are the criteria of assessment.

COURSE STRUCTURE AND METHODS

The course has been designed to be taken by students who remain in full-time employment during their studies. When the course was first started the students were typically from 25 to 35 years old but in recent years this has risen to 35 to 45. These people already hold senior positions in their companies and cannot be spared for long periods to attend courses at the university. To accommodate this the course comprises eight one-week intensive modules and a major project in industry. The duration of the course is between 18 and 24 months depending upon the needs and circumstances of individual students. Six of the eight modules are grouped in pairs and scheduled during the first three months of the course. The themes of these modules are:

- Learning and problem-solving skills
- Project definition, planning and control

- Working with people

- Engineering design

- Commercial background

- Communication skills.

The remaining two modules, which take place later, provide an opportunity for dealing with more advanced topics, including some which have been requested by the students.

During the first six modules a role play, known as the 'linking project', is carried out by the students in groups of between four and six. Each group undertakes the preparation of a tender to meet the requirements of a 'client' and of a business proposal for submission to their own 'management'. Thus the ideas and techniques which have been introduced during the modules can be practised in a safe environment. Mistakes can be made, analysed, and learnt from without the fear of the consequences which would be involved in a real project. The membership of the groups is fixed for the duration of the course so that they can function effectively as Action Learning Set Groups (Lessem, 1984). The pressure placed upon the students by the linking project drives each group rapidly through Tuckman's (1965) stages of group formation. Thus it quickly becomes an effective, performing, team whose members are committed to each other's success.

The greater part of the students' learning is derived from the experience of running one or more real projects in industry. The educational methodology of the course is therefore based upon Kolb's experiential learning cycle (Kolb and Fry, 1976) and this is explained to the students at the outset. The stages of the cycle are:

- Concrete experience

- Observations and reflections

- Formation of abstract concepts and generalizations

- Testing implications of concepts in new situations.

The last stage leads to fresh experiences and so the cycle continues. It is easy for the process of experiential learning to be interrupted by factors such as fear, inertia, ignorance, arrogance and low self-esteem. It is therefore very important that the course should provide a strongly supportive environment in which the students can learn from their own and each other's experiences. A key element in that support is the Set Group, already mentioned, which meets for up to a day about once every six weeks. The purpose of the group is to provide its members with mutual support, encouragement, criticism and advice to aid their learning and personal development (Lessem, 1984). If this is to happen effectively it is vital that the group members should meet in an atmosphere of openness and mutual trust. The group is supported in its aims by two tutors, one from the university and the other from industry, who act as facilitators. The students are encouraged to apply in their work what they have learnt during the modules and from private study, and to reflect upon the outcome. To promote the all-important reflective phase of Kolb's cycle they are asked to keep process diaries as personal and private records of their experience and of their reflections upon it. The emphasis on experiential learning is consonant with the objective that the students should become responsible for their own personal development both during and after the course.

ASSESSMENT

The assessment of students' progress and attainment is based upon a number of reports, two oral presentations and a dissertation. A clear distinction is made between formative and summative assessment. The general philosophy of the course is that what matters is the students' competence at the point of completion. They should not, therefore, be penalized for mistakes made during the course, provided that they learn from them. The greater part of the assessment carried out during the course is formative assessment. This aims to give the students as much feedback as possible about their progress so that they can achieve the best possible final results.

The reports used to provide formative assessments are:

● The main project definition and plan

● Two progress reports for the main project

● Two learning process reports.

The definition and plan and the progress reports provide tutors with the opportunity to comment in detail upon students' skills in planning and controlling their projects. The learning process reports which are based upon the students' process diaries are important because they encourage reflection and evaluation. They enable the tutors to comment particularly on the human aspects of the learning process and on the development of students' interpersonal skills. They also give the students the opportunity to practise the kind of writing they will need for their dissertations. This is especially necessary because they are unlikely to have done anything like it before.

The summative assessment is carried out in two stages: at the end of the linking project, and at the end of the main project. At the end of the linking project each group makes a presentation to the 'client' of a substantial tender document. The presentation is assessed for 10 per cent of the final marks. Subsequently each student writes a commentary on the process by which the group produced and presented its tender and this is assessed for 20 per cent of the final marks. At this stage more emphasis is placed upon critical reflection and learning than upon competence.

At the end of the main project each student submits a dissertation and makes a short public presentation of it to an audience which includes the examiners. The dissertation must make the case to the examiners that the objectives of the course have been attained. It is expected to incorporate the following elements:

- A description of the learning context

- A review of the evidence for learning and attainment against each objective supported by appendices containing documentary evidence

- A review of the whole experience of undertaking the course.

The assessment of this major element, which counts for 70 per cent of the final mark, is based entirely upon the dissertation. The presentation is used to provide the examiners with supplementary evidence and, sometimes, is used as a basis for choosing which candidates shall be given a *viva voce* examination. Our practice of allocating 70 per cent of the total marks to the dissertation submitted at the end of the course has been criticized on the grounds that it does not give sufficient credit for work done during the course. We believe that it is justified because the competence of the students at the end of the course must be the main criterion for the award of the degree. The majority of students pass at the first attempt with better marks for the dissertation than for the linking project. A few are required to revise the dissertation and are given guidance and tutorial support for that task and most of them pass at the second attempt. This supports the view that the allocation of 70 per cent of the marks to the dissertation is appropriate.

Both the linking project report and the dissertation are assessed using a mark sheet with sections for each of the eight course objectives and one for the style and presentation of the dissertation. The assessment of each piece of work is carried out independently by two examiners (neither of whom is the student's set group tutor). Ten marks are assigned to each course objective and 20 to the overall presentation of the work. In addition the examiners provide written comments against each heading. The students are given copies of the mark sheet at the start of the course so that they are aware of the assessment procedures.

Originally, no special guidance was given to the examiners, who used independent professional judgement. We found that the total marks awarded by two examiners frequently agreed with each other to within 5 per cent and we regard this as an acceptable level of accuracy for an assessment of this kind. In such cases we normally took the average of the two marks without further discussion. Where the two marks were further apart it was found that the examiners could generally agree on the marks to be awarded under each heading to within one mark of each other. The total marks were then usually within 5 per cent of each other as desired. This procedure, though reliable, depends heavily on the professional judgement of the examiners and on the established culture of the course and is opaque to the students.

In order to achieve greater uniformity between the marks awarded by different examiners it was necessary to find some way of specifying the criteria to be used for awarding the marks. Unfortunately the assessment of skills is more difficult than the assessment of knowledge because skills are multidimensional (Carter, 1985). The assessment must find a way of taking into account factors such as the difficulty of the task, the level of familiarity, the time available for carrying it out, the amount of help and supervision needed and the extent to which it was completed successfully. The final report on the Core Skills Project (Levy, 1987) suggested that competence involves three interrelated components concerned with:

- tasks (carrying out defined tasks in the workplace)
- task management (organizing tasks and activities within a working environment)
- the role/job environment (taking account of the context and environment, including the people within which the job takes place).

Methods were proposed for identifying the detailed skills involved. It was recognized that there was no reliable way of assessing the level of skilled performance and it was suggested that:

A new language of skill with which to describe more fully occupational competence would assist in the recording of competent performance in the workplace (*ibid*, p. 17).

The Core Skills Project was concerned with the comparatively low-level skills involved in the Youth Training Scheme (YTS). It is much more difficult to find a way of describing levels of skill in the much more complex tasks undertaken by professional engineers and managers.

Another report which tackled the question of learning outcomes and assessment in higher education concluded that:

> An outcome led approach requires staff to develop and use methods of assessment which measure achievements directly, but current assessment practice tends to neglect these questions of validity in favour of reliability, and many academic staff lack experience of appropriate approaches to assessment (Otter, 1992, p. 79).

It was recognized that considerable difficulties exist in finding a reliable approach to assessing skills at this level (*ibid*, pp. 50–51).

In order to try to reduce the variability between marks awarded by different examiners, we have devised the semantic scale shown in Table 8.2. This has been used for the last two years as the basis for awarding marks under each heading of assessment. On this scale a mark of 4 reflects basic competence, while marks of 8 and above are given for performance which is considered to be distinguished. The overall pass mark is 50 per cent so a candidate is unlikely to reach it without demonstrating competence in all categories of the assessment. The degree is awarded with distinction to candidates who achieve final marks of 70 per cent or better and they are likely to have been awarded 8 marks or more in several categories. Although no study of the effects of introducing the semantic scale has been carried out, our general impression is that it has resulted in a greater uniformity in the marks awarded by different examiners.

CONCLUSION

As a result of our experience with developing the MSc in Engineering Project Management we have concluded that, for such a competence-based course:

● It is best to specify the objectives in terms of a list of not more than ten generic skills, each of which can be demonstrated in a variety of ways according to the circumstances of the individual student.

● The course objectives must be communicated clearly to the students and all assessments must be carried out solely with reference to them. The marking scale for each objective should be no longer than ten points.

Table 8.2   *A semantic scale for assessment of competence*

Typical performance	Mark
Faultless performance under all circumstances.	10
Shows outstanding creativity and control in very difficult situations. Can give guidance to others.	9
Is aware of relevant theory and develops and adapts techniques to deal with new situations. Can give guidance to others.	8
Uses a range of techniques competently in complex situations. Offers insights and seeks out new techniques when necessary. Can give guidance to others.	7
Uses a range of techniques competently in complex situations. Seeks guidance when necessary.	6
Is aware of a range of techniques and can select an appropriate one and apply it correctly in straightforward situations. Requires guidance and occasional supervision.	5
Is aware of the main techniques and can apply them correctly in straightforward situations. Should seek assistance when necessary. Needs supervision.	4
Is aware of the main techniques but needs some help to apply them to straightforward situations. Needs close supervision.	3
Tends to know one technique and tries to apply it to all situations. Needs constant guidance, oversight and direction.	2
Often shows ignorance of basic techniques or misapplies them.	1
Has no idea at all of what he is doing, or has supplied no evidence.	0

- The marks awarded independently by experienced examiners are commonly in close agreement with each other and it is easy to achieve agreement to within one mark on any objective by discussion.

- The consistency of marking can be improved still further by using a semantic scale such as that shown in Table 8.2 to guide the awarding of marks, provided that it is written using language and concepts which are natural for assessment of competence in the field.

The final results achieved in this way are generally in line with a subjective judgement of each student's attainment and place within the class. We believe that the procedures which we have developed are valid, reliable and simple to use.

Chapter 9

A Case Study in Project-based Learning and Competency Profiling

Alan Beattie

TEACHING AND LEARNING ABOUT HEALTH PROMOTION

In the past few years something called the settings-based approach to the practice of health promotion has attracted a great deal of professional interest (Baric, 1993), and it has become a central focus for the development of policy and practice, both internationally (in the work of the World Health Organization) and nationally (in the health promotion agencies of the four countries of the UK). At local level it is seen in new initiatives such as the health promoting school (SHEG, 1990; Young and Williams, 1990); the health promoting hospital (HEA, 1993; NHSE, 1994); and the health promoting workplace (Jones, 1992; Philo *et al.*, 1993). Such initiatives typically attempt to review and bring together interventions to improve health across a wide range of topics – say, action on smoking and alcohol drinking, healthy eating, coronary prevention, the management of stress, the promotion of sexual health – so as to encourage a more holistic view of health. They also typically try to set an agenda for action at the corporate level: seeking organizational change at the level of the systems and policies in an institution that may create or contribute to personal ill-health, or which may thwart our efforts as individuals to take better care of ourselves.

To anyone involved in teaching and learning about health promotion as an academic field of study, the settings approach is highly attractive. It provides an excellent incentive to review what we know about good practice in health promotion on a broad front. At the same time it offers a challenging test-case for the development of theoretical frameworks in health promotion. For instance, the settings approach is in several respects a useful example of the so-called ecological perspective, which is one of the frameworks that health promotion has drawn on in attempting to move beyond the biomedical perspective that has focused primarily on getting individuals to change their lifestyles. A national project on 'the health promoting college', funded by the Health Education Authority (HEA), has since 1988 explored this approach in further education settings (O'Donnell and Gray, 1993), and at the University College of St Martin in Lancaster since Summer 1993, we have been developing a similar line of work within the higher education setting.

For example, on a new undergraduate BA course in Health Promotion (the first of its kind in the UK), we give students an opportunity for small-scale project work on the campus in a module (HP201) on 'Health promotion theory and practice'. This offers a modest practicum for experiential learning, a chance to try out approaches and to acquire transferable skills within a relatively safe and protected environment. The projects that the students undertake give them and us a chance to see ideas and methods being tried out in highly creative (and low cost) ways. Like the HEA health promoting college project, we have chosen to explore the range of possible health promotion activities with the help of a 'strategic map' (Beattie, 1991) which offers a way of handling the multiple and competing definitions of practice in health promotion. Our attempt to use this conceptual framework illustrates some of the difficult issues that arise in moving towards competency-oriented learning and its assessment.

MAPPING THE MULTIPLE COMPETENCES FOR HEALTH PROMOTION PRACTICE

Perhaps the foremost difficulty is defining the competences in question. The Care Sector Consortium (CSC) has drafted a 'Functional map of health and social care' which it appears will form the basis for the development by the HEA of a definitive statement of occupational standards and competences for health promotion (Rolls, 1994). But successive drafts of the CSC map seem to exemplify the tendency identified by Otter (1992) for occupational competences to over-emphasize technical/functional aspects of practice and to neglect the ethical, at both personal and professional levels. Issitt has suggested that the technical-rational approach to mapping occupational standards and competences – seen in the NCVQ's 'functional analysis' – may be ill-equipped to deal with professional practice in health promotion because work in this field is highly contested and may fall largely within the indeterminate zones of practice (Issitt, 1994; Issitt and Woodward, 1992). Indeed there is a large and fast-growing literature on the diverse forms that contemporary health promotion can take and on the social values that are at stake in these different forms (Beattie, 1991; Bunton and MacDonald, 1992; Caplan, 1993; Caplan and Holland, 1990; Downie *et al.*, 1990; Draper *et al.*, 1979; Kelly *et al.*, 1993; Rawson, 1993; Tones and Tilford, 1994).

For example, 'health information giving' has often been seen as the only – or the most appropriate – form for health promotion. 'Personal counselling for health' has probably begun to move into the mainstream of professional health competences. 'Administrative action for health', where health expertise is used in lobbying and campaigning for changes in the policies and systems that affect health, has an honourable but chequered history within public health, and is arguably now coming to the forefront in the context of the settings-based approach. 'Community development for health', in which the practitioner helps groups of people who have similar health concerns or are in similar circumstances to come together to take joint action to improve their health prospects, is only just beginning to figure on the map of health promotion practice to any significant degree. Considerable tensions often arise between different ways of doing the job of health promotion, for example between prescriptive and negotiated approaches, and between action focused on individuals and that focused on collective systems.

So, in defining competences in health promotion, there is no unproblematic and clear-cut body of skills or expertise readily available for transmission to students. On the contrary, a grasp of the conflicts and controversies (scientific, practical, ethical and political) that are the hallmark of work in health promotion is an inescapable foundation for successful professional practice (Beattie, 1991). It may be vital for students themselves, as part of their learning, to deliberate and debate what is deemed to count as health promotion competence.

The scheme of assessment that I have devised for use within our HP201 course is an attempt to draw attention to the complexity and multiplicity of the strategic options available for health promotion in practice. It revolves around a portfolio of competences (see Document 9.1) which is generated in a systematic way from my four-fold matrix for the analysis of 'strategic choices' in health promotion (see Figure 9.1).

A major challenge in using competency maps as a basis for teaching about health promotion is to go beyond seeing the strategic alternatives as mutually exclusive. Effective health promotion practice may often (perhaps increasingly) require 'professional artistry' – being able to switch between different approaches, or to combine them in novel and creative ways, according to the problem in hand. As Runciman suggested, speaking in the context of competency-based approaches to teaching nursing studies:

competency (is) a multifaceted concept with both finite and global interpretations: the finite definition equates it with a behavioural objective; the global definition embraces 'performance of complex tasks in specified real-world settings'. Detailed behavioural objective-

Mode
Prescriptive

Health information giving. Role = instructor and persuader: seeking to remedy deficits	Administrative action for health. Role = custodian: seeking to guard and protect against environmental risks

Focus Individual ————————————————————— Collective

Personal counselling for health. Role = counsellor: seeking to empower the troubled individual	Community development for health. Role = activist: seeking to mobilize and support embattled groups

Negotiated

Figure 9.1   *A matrix of health promotion strategies*

type statements... may still be relevant, particularly in the early stages of a programme. In addition, however, statements of learning outcomes for the later stages of an educational programme, which capture higher levels of learning and performance in complex and varied nursing situations, will also be necessary and may be an even greater challenge for programme designers (Runciman, 1990, p. 12).

In HP201, I encourage students to build up a broad and flexible grasp of the multiple forms of health promotion, and to work towards a pluralistic, multi-paradigm approach to practice. In this direction I believe lies a way of handling the puzzle of good practice in situations that are uncertain and often conflictual, where there may be deep divides between different views as to what might count as good practice (Twinn, 1991).

DESIGNING A MANY-SIDED CURRICULUM FOR HEALTH PROMOTION STUDIES

Arguably, the teaching and learning processes required for contemporary health promotion are most effectively achieved by providing a deliberate mix and variety of study and assessment opportunities with sufficient open-endedness to avoid predictability. My own approach to this aspect of course design can be summed up as follows:

(if) courses are to be adequate for preparing ... for practice in the 21st Century, they will need to be put together in ways that boldly juxtapose different orientations to curriculum design. This will require new and more complex patterns for the structuring and sequencing of courses – matched by an appropriate mix of teaching and learning methods and an appropriate mixed menu of modes of student assessment (Beattie, 1990, p. 33).

Documents 9.1–9.6 show how the assessment arrangements for this course are organized so as to encourage students to develop and apply knowledge for the different areas of competence indicated in Figure 9.1. The scheme of assessment for HP201 is used to steer learning; its structure and sequence offer the students routes through the expertise that is required for the settings approach to health promotion.

REVIEWING STUDENT WORK

We use the matrix in Figure 9.1 to spur consideration of the questions:

- What could be done to make St. Martin's College a more health-promoting environment?

- What could you do to make St. Martin's College a more health-promoting environment? Are there specific interests, ideas, skills you can offer?

Working in groups, the 1993–4 cohort students came up with the lines of work shown in Figure 9.2 (their tabulations of which reflect their own creative adaptations of Figure 9.1).

In work of this sort, the course and its concomitant assessment menu provide a focus for the development of key insights and skills for the practice of health promotion, and for discussion and debate about the issues of personal and professional ethics surrounding intervention in the lifestyles and living environments of higher education students. In summer term 1994, displays and events related to this work were brought together in an open day on St Martin's as a health promoting college. In addition to presentations that students undertook in the public eye, much of their activity took the form of lobbying and campaigning behind the scenes, only some of which was reported on in the exhibition.

Topic 1: Promoting sexual health

health-risk advice	educational/rational	self-empowerment	action for change
– take it or leave it Run topic days Provide HP201 stall/cubby-hole at SU shop, GP, medical centre, family planning clinic, welfare office	*– to raise personal awareness* *– to enable decision making* Run 'attitude change' groups, eg, lesbian, gay, bisexual	*– to relate on deeper and more intimate level* *– to examine self-esteem, self-worth and effect change* College counselling Women's group Domestic violence sufferers and sexual abuse survivors	*– to raise national/ local awareness* *– to effect local/ community change* 'Bitter pill' campaign 'Age of consent' campaign

Topic 2: Promoting healthy eating

health-risk advice	self-empowerment	action for change (top-down)	action for change (bottom-up)
Run awareness weeks with leaflets/posters Medical centre Welfare officer Healthy diet advice	Counselling groups/ societies SU activities Christian Union activities Self-awareness/ acceptance and assertion training	College policy Equal opportunities policies Chaplaincy policy	Groups/societies SU activities Healthy food options

Topic 3: Promoting exercise and fitness

health-risk advice	educational/rational	self-empowerment	action for change
Run campaign days, eg, no smoking Advice via College health service Heart health awareness	Educate for healthy lifestyle Educate for stress management Show how to organize study time Illustrate benefits of changing lifestyle patterns	Build self-esteem Provide assertiveness training	Provide exercise opportunities, eg, at lunchtimes Provide fitness assessments

Figure 9.2   *Frameworks for health promotion practice*

Document 9.1   *The portfolio of personal/professional development*

The most important feature of this double module course is that you select a Health Promotion (HP) area or topic on which you believe action is justified and feasible in the St. Martin's setting; and that you try out your proposed action and report on it. The action is intended to be absolutely and entirely for real.

Our overall aims in the St. Martin's as a Health Promoting College (SM/HPC!) project are to:

- achieve tangible and practical health gains, for students and perhaps for staff as well

- help bring about changes in the College as an institution that make health gains sustainable

- practise and demonstrate the highest standards of ethical and effective practice in health promotion

- draw on relevant theory-and-practice and research-and-development from wider examples of the settings-based approach to health promotion e.g. schools, hospitals, workplaces, etc

- link with and to exchange ideas with the HEA national project on The Health Promoting College

- disseminate our findings to practitioners and academics in health promotion throughout the UK

The SM/HPC project offers a vehicle for engaging in problem-solving activities in health promotion, and gives you the opportunity to develop basic competences that enable you to move from novice to expert in health promotion work. By the end of the module you should all be knowledgeable doers in health promotion, each of you able to provide your own individual portfolio of evidence of achievement in several domains.

For assessment purposes, you are required to produce for HP201 (as a double module) a total of about 8000 words, which you should see as adding up to your cumulative portfolio of evidence of personal and professional development. In summary:

Coursework 1 is about planning a health promotion project in the higher education setting.

Coursework 2 is about action for health promotion in the higher education setting.

In preparing your portfolio of evidence of achievement you are advised to monitor your own progress to the fullest extent possible by making reference to the checklists that are set out in documents 9.2–9.6 below. These give you guidance in each of the following domains.

1. Key theoretical understandings for justifying and planning health promotion

2. Essential practical skills for delivering health promotion

3a. Awareness of your own personal values and feelings as they affect your health promotion work

3b. Awareness of wider social and cultural controversies (current affairs) that shape health promotion

Document 9.2 *Coursework 1: Planning a health promotion project in the higher education setting*

You should use this piece of work to develop and present the case for action on a selected topic in the context of St. Martin's as a Health Promoting College (SM/HPC). You should draw on library work – citing relevant textbooks, research reports, or other sources – to help you formulate your argument. You should also, as far as is feasible, carry out small-scale first-hand inquiries (observations, conversations, interviews, document analysis) to provide evidence to support your views as to why your chosen topic is important in the College setting. In this respect you may think of yourself as working like an investigative journalist.

This is your first opportunity to pull together evidence to show key theoretical understandings for justifying and planning health promotion (the competences set out in document 9.4, below). You MUST show very clearly that you have thought about the issues involved in selecting a health promotion strategy and approach; and show that you understand what are the theoretical foundations and practical implications of the particular model(s) that you decide to use for planning purposes (see document 9.4, subsection 1.1 Health Promotion Models and Planning). You must also make a feature of recent advances in health sciences relevant to your chosen topic (see subsection 1.2 Biopsychosocial Foundations of Health Promotion). You could draw on elements of HP101 (from last year) to do so; and you may find it helpful to incorporate some information or ideas from HP203 (Environment and Health), and/or from HP204 (Sociology of Health). You may also choose to develop some ideas and arguments that relate to various contexts in the planning of health promotion work, such as those set out in document 9.4, subsections 1.3 Health Management Studies; 1.4 Social and Community Studies; 1.5 Social Ethics.

Think in terms of building up a file which may include a review of relevant academic literature; an analysis/critique of current policy/practice; and also such items as news clippings, quotes from interviews, observation notes etc.

You will be invited to present your ideas (as far as they have developed by then) to a small, invited, internal audience in the last week of term 1. On that occasion, the main thing is to present your thoughts and argue persuasively what it is that you believe should and could be done about your topic/issue. The feedback that you get on this occasion should be a highly valuable input to your submission of Coursework 1.

The final submitted Coursework 1 should add up to a maximum of 3000 words, and will count for 40% of the marks for HP201. Whatever format it takes, it should be written in a lively style, intended to communicate with wider audiences in the College. It should include a 100 word precis/summary in broadsheet style, of the sort that could capture the attention of busy people who might come across it in the Union, a common room, etc. Beyond that it could consist of 1 long piece or of 2 or 3 shorter pieces (for example a magazine article; the text for a display or leaflet; letters to VIPs; a press release; etc). In this way you can look ahead to term 2 and Coursework 2, and begin to develop your evidence of competences in the areas set out in documents 9.4 and 9.6.

Document 9.3   *Coursework 2: Action for health promotion in the higher education setting*

You should use this piece of work to prepare, try out and report on small-scale activities designed to take forward the SM/HPC project. It is your opportunity to present evidence to show the competences in the domains set out in sections 2 and 3 below, and probably to revisit those in section 1. Please do without fail check yourself against them!

Coursework item 2 should add up to a maximum of 5000 words and will count for 60% of the total marks for HP201. This coursework submission should be your own first-hand account of your own attempt at health promotion in action: what exactly you were trying to do, what you did in the event, and what you learned from this experience. This is an action-report, and it should be written (like Coursework 1) in a lively style. Again, as for Coursework 1, please include a 100 word precis/summary in broadsheet style to capture the attention of staff and students across the College. Beyond this, the report need not necessarily be in one single unitary form: it could contain a number of diverse items, such as the following:

1. A review of learning resources or other materials that you've looked at during your project

2. A letter to students following on in subsequent years, who may be involved in what could become an annual update on how SMC is doing as a health-promoting environment. Figure out what you can tell them that is really useful, pithy, thought-provoking, personally inspiring, compulsive reading!

3. Edited excerpts from your own personal learning logbook (you should be thinking about starting to write those diary entries very soon indeed!) plus comments on those excerpts

4. Brief synopses/abstracts of work that you've carried out for other modules during the year – indicating how/why it's relevant to the SM/HPC project. For example HP202 might give you a chance to develop in depth some aspect of field research and data-gathering related – if you wish – to your chosen HPC activity. HP205 might give you a chance to carry out a small-scale exercise in 1:1 inter-action and in small group interaction – likewise, if you wish, related to your chosen HPC activity

5. A review of the responses to letters you've sent to important sta-keholders, power-holders, budget-holders, intended to elicit policy information, or persuade re policy change, or invite to discuss policy

6. A revised and tested topic pamphlet, leaflet or other similar hand-out for general circulation in college

Document 9.4 *A set of key theoretical understandings for health promotion*

Submit written work to show evidence of at least TWO areas of understanding, including BOTH 1.1 + 1.2 below + (possibly) any others from subsections 1.3–1.5.

1.1 Health Promotion Models and Planning

Discuss the merits and shortcomings as they apply to your topic at SMC, of different approaches to HP planning e.g. (a) Beattie's 4-fold grid (Figure 9.1) (b) Tannahill's 3-circle map (c) Greene's PRECEDE.

1.2 Biopsychosocial Foundations of Health Promotion

Review current evidence that relates to the case for taking action in an IHE (Institute of Higher Education) on your selected topic

1.3 Health Management Studies

- Consider the lessons that can be learned, for HP in IHEs, from HP initiatives in other settings

- Discuss the factors that need to be taken into account in corporate planning/action for HP in IHEs

- Show how social policy (e.g. current legal/fiscal/economic changes) may set limits to HP in IHEs

- Assess the contribution to the development of HP policy and practice in IHEs of any one of the following: (a) World Health Organization (b) HEA/HPAW/SHEB (c) NUS

- Consider the issues associated with local voluntary organisations contributing to HP in IHEs

- Examine how far current theory and practice related to HEA2000 policies may inform HP in IHEs

- Show how an 'ecological' model for health may inform HP in IHEs

1.4 Social and Community Studies

- Review the significance for HP in IHEs of any one current social movement

- Discuss the contribution of the church and pastoral activity to the development of HP in IHEs

- Consider how far HP in IHEs can benefit from any of the following skills (a) neighbourhood work (b) community social work (c) outreach work

- Assess the significance, for HP in IHEs, of radical adult education practices

- Review the techniques that may be used to increase student participation in HP in IHEs

1.5 Social Ethics

- Prepare a commentary on ethical challenges that arise in developing HP in a Church College

- Consider whether there are circumstances in which it could be considered legitimate to adopt, as strategies in HP in IHEs: (a) persuasion (b) coercion

- Review the arguments for and against compliance, 'informed choice' or empowerment as aims for HP in IHEs

- Review the social–political values that may impinge on the selection of a strategy for HP in IHEs

Document 9.5 *A range of essential practical skills for health promotion*

Submit a file of work that shows at least TWO competences in use. Each should be from a different subsection (2.1–2.4 set out below).

2.1 Information-giving

● Adapt or write, and assess, a leaflet, factsheet or other source of structured information

● Prepare, set up and assess an exhibition or poster or other graphic display; organise, run and assess a stall at a College or SU event

● Run a seminar on your HP topic, with speakers from both inside and outside (and for and against)

● Select, use, and assess a video or other audiovisual resource

● Produce or adapt, and assess, a package of self-instruction learning materials

2.2 Interpersonal and experiential learning

● Carry out and report on a role-play or game or simulation

● Devise or adapt, use and assess drama /theatre methods; e.g. a small-scale theatre event

● Select, use and assess one or more named devices for structuring a personal counselling session (e.g. life-space diagrams; time lines; etc)

● Negotiate individual learning contracts with a small sample of clients

● Run and monitor one or more developmental group work or focus group sessions

● Run and monitor one or more sessions using values clarification techniques

2.3 Lobbying and campaigning

● Prepare and disseminate an action report, based on a survey related to a health issue at SMC

● Organise and run a public meeting (to discuss action on your health topic)

● Write letters (on your case for action) to figures in positions of authority/ influence in the College

● Submit an 'alternative statement' or critique in response to a recent policy document from a named agency

● Get together a petition among SMC students and/or staff on your chosen issue

- Use desk-top publishing facilities to produce a newsletter, bulletin or broadsheet re HP at SMC

- Put together a 'press release' to raise issues around HP at SMC

- Put together a 'social action broadcast' to raise issues around HP at SMC

2.4 Community development and networking

- Negotiate access to a College group (e.g. women's group; eating disorders group; etc), contribute to its work, and report on what you have been able to do

- Invite in, and undertake joint work with, a local voluntary agency (e.g. MIND; MENCAP); and produce a report on it

Document 9.6 *A sampler of personal and social awareness in health promotion*

Submit a personal-social file to show how your own awareness of personal issues and wider social affairs in HP has developed and changed during the HP201 project. This is a free-choice activity, but should encompass both the personal and the social; some suggestions are given below in subsections 3.1 and 3.2

As a source for this, you are recommended to keep a reflective diary (or journal or commonplace book or some other form of 'personal learning' log), and/or perhaps try out some autobiographical writing.

The crucial thing is to use this to write notes on the experiences you find most troublesome, pressing or challenging in any way – particular incidents or episodes (horror stories? breakthroughs?) that you feel compelled to write down; or particular areas of awareness or insight (brilliant ideas and brainwaves) that you feel prompted to record in (say) a letter home, to future students etc. You should expect to pull out extracts from all this, to make up the personal-social file that you submit.

3.1 Awareness of personal issues related to health promotion

- Review changes in your personal stance regarding information-giving and/or fear arousal methods

- Comment on the impact of your studies on your own 'self-appraisal' of your health and/or lifestyle

- Review your personal stance re giving/receiving personal help/counselling in major life transitions

- Review your personal stance re legal/fiscal/environmental interventions in personal/public health

- Review your personal stance regarding anti-sexist/anti-racist/self-help perspectives in HP

3.2 Awareness of social affairs related to health promotion

- Trace how your own HP issue is dealt with in the media, and set up your own cuttings/jottings file

- Maintain awareness of current national/local political debates relevant to your selected HP topic

- Monitor the activities of one or more relevant local voluntary health self-help groups

The 1993-4 cohort also produced a string of detailed recommendations for future work on the health promoting campus; and the new
1994–5 cohort are responding to these, as well as having many new ideas
of their own. For my part, I would add that another practical item of work
for the future is to adopt and adapt the same portfolio of competences for
use in other contexts. We are already using it (selectively) for students
doing their work placements in health promotion. We are planning to
extend its use into other levels of the health promotion course, both
lower and higher; and yet another challenge is to use the portfolio to
guide students on other professional courses such as youth and community work; teaching; nursing; the therapies. But I would also add that
there is immense scope and challenge for future research related to
issues of theory that arise in this work. Above all, the competences
portfolio itself merits further theoretical and empirical exploration.
Beyond this, the processes by which individual students acquire a grasp of
complex and diverse competences (like those in the portfolio) are very
inadequately theorized, and it might be particularly illuminating to
explore these in terms of 'cycles of experiential learning' (for example,
Edwards and Brunton, 1993; Fish *et al.*, 1990). In turn the exercise of
professional artistry in health promotion is imperfectly understood, and
it might be fruitful to examine the applicability (to this area of work) of
'imaginization' as a strategy for creative practice within organizational
settings (for example, Morgan, 1986).

CONCLUSION

As Boys, Winter, and Tomlinson and Saunders, for example, have shown
(see Chapters 2, 4 and 5 in this volume), it is no simple matter to arrive at
a view of what it means to be competent in an area, a theme well
developed by Barnett (1994) and in greater detail by Eraut (1994). Here,
a model has been offered for mapping the major competences in health
promotion. But it is far from sufficient just to have such a model. Student
learning crucially depends upon the assessment activities associated with
a course or programme. Our experience on HP201 shows that generating
an assessment menu from a model of competences can be effective in
guiding students into and through the field of health promotion practice,
and getting them to work on the key professional competences in the
process. A notable feature of this model is that the competences are
interconnected, just as they are in the real-life role. This takes us well
beyond the atomized, reductionist and mechanistic approaches sometimes seen in competency-based programmes of study. Rather, our
students have to weave together the set of competences, always with

questions about values and ethics in mind. The key to this has been a focus on the development and assessment of competences through real-life health promotion work. In this respect, then, the St Martin's as a health promoting college project has allowed us, on a degree-level course, to adopt an approach to the assessment of competence that in some ways echoes (and in some ways challenges) the work of the NCVQ.

Acknowledgements

I would like to thank Marion Nuttall for her support in getting this project going, and the HP201 students (1993–4 and 1994–5) for their energy in doing it.

Chapter 10

The Development of Skills through Peer-assessment

James Price and Hugh Cutler

BACKGROUND

In 1992 the geography department at St Martin's College introduced a new geography degree which incorporated an innovative and modern scheme of assessment. The new degree demands peer- and self-assessment of seminars and presentations in all three years, as well as requiring students to produce reports, do projects and undertake other assessment activities.

A number of reasons led to the decision to make this 'root and branch' change to our degree programme. Some were internal to the institution, while others were responses to external developments, such as Enterprise in Higher Education, the growing interest in flexible learning and the general debate within higher education about assessment, competences and vocational education and training. Finally, there were developments within the pedagogy of geography in higher education, most notably the work of the geography education unit at Oxford Polytechnic, as it then was. With the move in higher education to give students responsibility for their own learning and development, we felt that all of these factors were leading us to develop a new system of assessment. The end product was our new degree programme. Table 10.1 summarizes its assessment arrangements.

PEER- AND SELF-ASSESSMENT

We already had structures to develop a range of transferable skills and personal competences, including study skills. These tended however to be limited to written skills and quantitative skills. We felt that it was now time to emphasize other skills, particularly those related to presentation and organization and to develop further students' teamwork and

150

Table 10.1 *Assessment arrangements in the new geography degree*

Assessment Type	Assessment Mode		
	Self-	*Peer-*	*Staff (M = Monitoring)*
Examination			*
Essay	*		*
Seminar	*	*	M
Project:			
Individual	*		*
Group	*	*	M
Oral Presentation	*	*	M
Report/Review	*		*
Practical/Field File	*		M
IT File	*		*
Field Course File	*		*
Portfolio			*
Dissertation Proposal			*
Dissertation			*
Placement			
Proposal			*
Diary	*		M
Report	*	*	*

research skills. Conditions in higher education since the 1980s have been suited to the overt development of independent learning and to the concept of the student as autonomous learner. One justification for assessing oral presentations and seminars is that it also aids the development of presentational and organizational skills. In order to check upon the development of these particular skills it is necessary to make use of assessment of students by their peers, that is to say, to use peer-assessment. Accordingly, presentations and seminars have been built into each of the three years of the geography programme. Performances are judged against a set of criteria, reproduced in Figure 10.1.

Presentations and seminar performances are peer-assessed, but at the same time the students making the presentations fill in self-appraisal

University College of St Martin. Geography Department

PEER APPRAISAL FORM: PRESENTATION

Title:
Course Number:
Students:

A. SUBJECT MATTER

1. Theoretical basis	5	4	3	2	1	0	
Clear use of theory/ concepts	❑	❑	❑	❑	❑	❑	No use of theory/ concepts

Comments

2. Content	5	4	3	2	1	0	
Full explanation of the topic	❑	❑	❑	❑	❑	❑	Inadequate explanation

Comments

3. Organization	5	4	3	2	1	0	
Subject matter is well integrated	❑	❑	❑	❑	❑	❑	Subject matter is disorganized and muddled

Comments

B. PRESENTATION

4. Creativity	5	4	3	2	1	0	
Wide range of approaches, imaginative, interesting	❑	❑	❑	❑	❑	❑	Narrow range of approaches, dull, predictable

Comments

5. Communication	5	4	3	2	1	0	
Clear, well presented, convincing	❑	❑	❑	❑	❑	❑	Unclear, poorly presented, unconvincing

Comments

6. Teamwork   5   4   3   2   1   0

Cooperative   ❏   ❏   ❏   ❏   ❏   ❏   No cooperation, looks

involvement of full   like one person's work

team clearly evident

Comments

Score (out of 30) _____

Figure 10.1   *Peer-appraisal form*

forms. This requires them to reflect upon their achievement by giving their own presentation a mark and by justifying it. The self-assessment form is shown in Figure 10.2.

A discussion of the degree to which this approach to the assessment of some core competences has proved successful forms the basis of the rest of this chapter. For this purpose we have chosen to describe the process of peer- and self-assessment in two second-year courses and one third-year course.

THE ASSESSMENT PROCESS

G201 and G202 are two 'core' second-year courses which provide an introduction to human and physical geography respectively. Their assessment arrangements are very similar in that each gives 50 per cent to a formal examination; 30 per cent to essays and 20 per cent to seminar/ presentations which are peer-assessed (20 per cent in 201 for two seminars and 10 per cent in 202 for one seminar. The remaining 10 per cent in 202 is for a field file, which is self- and tutor-assessed).

In order to produce seminar groups the class (58 in 1994) is divided into four equally sized groups labelled 1–4. Each of them is sub-divided into four small groups, the majority of which are friendship groups. The seminars are then organized into cycles of four weeks with each group knowing when they are to lead a seminar and also the title of it. In the weeks when presentations take place, there are two seminars presented by groups of three to four students.

At the end of each presentation and after questions and discussions each presenter fills in a self-assessment sheet and suggests a mark (with reasons) and all students and the member of staff present fill in a peer-assessment sheet. The student 'marks' are averaged to give 50 per cent of the final mark and the staff mark provides the other 50 per cent. No

University College of St Martin. Geography Department

Self-Appraisal Form: Presentation/Seminar

Title:

Course number:

Student:

A. My presentation/seminar contribution is worth the following mark _____%

B. Reasons for the mark
   Tick which of the following features you felt were good in your contribution to the seminar/presentation and make any comments you wish to support the mark you have given yourself:

                                                                        Comments

1. Verbal presentation

2. Overhead

3. Poster/handouts

4. Contribution to class discussion

5. Research

6. Other (eg)

C. In the view of your tutor (where relevant) your seminar presentation was worth _____% because

Figure 10.2   *Self-appraisal form*

marks are released to the students until the seminar paper based on the presentation is provided for the use of the other students.

In the third year there are two differences. In the first instance the group to whom the presentation is made is smaller and the student audience is usually better read so that a genuine seminar debate often results from the paper given. Secondly, the peer-appraisal mark is an average of the student marks with no contribution by the staff member. In fact, in some cases the member of staff is not present and the students deliver a presentation/seminar, mark it and provide the tutor with the peer- and self-appraisal forms and the agreed mark.

In addition to developing a new range of skills in our students it should be remembered that as a form of flexible learning it does save on staff time. This form of assessment increases student independence, gets them fully involved in the learning process, makes them discuss/work together and considerably improves their research skills. The opportunity is provided by tutors for students to discuss their presentations beforehand and to be given help with courses and access to equipment such as video recorders. There is less need for tutor feedback and, in year three, no tutor marking. Tutor time is restricted to producing the average mark for the presentations from the 'anonymous' peer-assessment sheets, and to checking upon the handing in of the written paper.

THE STUDENT EXPERIENCE

Part of the analysis that follows is based on a questionnaire specifically dealing with seminars and presentations given to students 18 months into the operation of the new degree scheme. Fifty questionnaires were completed by second-year students (who all had experience of groundwork in this area during their first-year course) and 32 questionnaires were completed by third-year students. The questionnaire is printed as Figure 10.3 and shows the raw scores for the combined 82 responses.

Although more students agreed with the views that marks achieved in seminars/presentations were both fair and accurate than disagreed, more students perceived the marks as fair than as accurate. Seventy-three per cent of students thought that marks for seminars/presentations should be moderated by a member of staff. This proportion was approximately the same for the second-year cohort, where moderation takes place, and for the third year, where there is no staff moderation and less staff involvement.

In comparison with their previous year's performance, 85 per cent of students felt that they had gained in confidence and 80 per cent that they had improved their seminar/presentation skills. These views were

Geography Department

SEMINAR/PRESENTATION QUESTIONNAIRE

Please will you complete the following questionnaire as fully and as accurately as
you can. For the following statements please ring the appropriate number:

(Combined Year 2/3 raw scores)

	Strongly Agree				Strongly Disagree
1. Marks achieved in seminars/presentations are fair	1	2	3	4	5
	7	28	29	15	3
2. Marks achieved in seminars/presentations are accurate	1	2	3	4	5
	2	28	31	18	3
3. Marks achieved in seminars/presentations should be moderated by a member of staff	1	2	3	4	5
	35	25	18	4	0
4. My confidence in giving a seminar/ presentation has improved since last academic year	1	2	3	4	5
	30	40	7	3	2
5. My skill in giving a seminar/presentation has improved since last academic year	1	2	3	4	5
	20	46	14	2	0
6. I participate more in seminars than I did last academic year	1	2	3	4	5
	18	29	26	8	1
7. I have had sufficient guidance in giving seminars/presentations	1	2	3	4	5
	10	26	28	15	3
8. I am happy being assessed by my peer(s)	1	2	3	4	5
	12	37	19	7	7
9. I am confident in assessing my peer(s)	1	2	3	4	5
	13	35	23	8	3

10. I feel my assessment of my peer(s) is
    accurate

1	2	3	4	5
13	**28**	**31**	**7**	**3**

11. I am confident in assessing my own
    seminar/presentation

1	2	3	4	5
10	**37**	**26**	**8**	**1**

12. I am accurate in assessing my own seminar/
    presentation

1	2	3	4	5
3	**40**	**30**	**5**	**4**

Figure 10.3   *Extract from the seminar presentation questionnaire and summary of findings*

particularly strong amongst the third year, being 97 per cent and 91 per cent respectively. Sixty-four per cent of second years but only 47 per cent of third years agreed that they participated more in seminars/presentations than in the previous year. Twice as many students agreed that they had had sufficient guidance in giving seminars/presentations than disagreed.

The main findings from the open-response section (not shown in Figure 10.3) were:

- 60 per cent of students were happy at being assessed by their peers with only 17 per cent being unhappy

- 59 per cent were confident in assessing their peers

- 50 per cent felt that their assessment of their peers was accurate

- key seminar presentation skills were – ability to organize material (78 per cent), use of voice (68 per cent), use of visual aids (59 per cent) and confidence (50 per cent) and teamwork (34 per cent)

- at least a third of students thought that they had improved in confidence, organization of material and use of voice

- 9 per cent of students felt that they had not developed any skills since the previous academic year but two-thirds of the students indicated that there were no skills that they had not improved from the previous year

- reasons why skills had not improved were attributed to their personality and confidence and, in some cases, to lack of preparation

● few comments were added to the pro-forma but can be summarized as a student recognition of the importance and relevance of seminars and presentations in the assessment strategy of the degree, allied to a concern that the techniques and processes of peer-assessment need refinement.

From this general review it would appear that the student experience of seminar and presentation assessment in the department is a positive one but, since neither cohort has experienced the complete three-year operation of the assessment strategy, full judgement has to be deferred.

MODERATION AND RELIABILITY

During the process of validating the 1992 geography degree it was agreed that elements of peer-assessment should not constitute more than 20 per cent of the assessment of any unit, lest any student be unfairly advantaged or disadvantaged. Staff moderation was therefore in-built.

One way of attempting to determine the need for this comes from examining the variation between marks achieved through peer- and self-assessment and those given by the member of staff moderating. Early in the operation of the new degree in 1992 there was clear evidence that student peer-assessment was above staff assessment, often by a margin of 10. Moderation reduced the final mark to within 5 of the staff mark. Although not fully explored to date, there is evidence to indicate that after a year's experience the discrepancy between student and staff assessments tends to be lower, more often less than 5 marks. During this time the pro-forma for self-assessment of seminars/presentations was refined and this may have contributed to narrowing of the discrepancy. Increasing student experience and greater critical awareness may also be seen as possible contributing factors.

Comparison of peer- and self-assessment marks with others in the student's profile cannot directly be used as a measure of reliability. Since, for example, self-assessed seminars and staff-assessed essays are measuring differing skills and learning outcomes there need not necessarily be any relationship between the two. Marks obtained by individual students for the two seminar/presentations in G201 correlated significantly with those obtained in G202, whereas the essay marks in the two units did not correlate with each other. In both G201 and G202 there was no significant correlation between seminar mark and essay performance. On the other hand, for both units seminar marks correlated significantly with overall unit marks, whereas essay marks did not. Precise interpretation of these relationships requires data for further cohorts but the following conclusions could be ventured. First, the seminars and presentations are assessing skills more than knowledge and these skills are transferable from unit to unit. Second, the essay is assessing knowledge rather more obviously than skill, and in the two different areas of human and physical geography students' preferences and knowledge bases vary. The close correlation between the seminar mark and the overall unit mark is more difficult to explain in view of the low weighting given to the seminar/ presentation mark and requires further exploration.

CONCLUSION

This chapter has given an example of a departmental approach to curriculum development which has seen progress in the promotion and assessment of core competences through the normal business of good geography teaching. The value of continuing enquiry into the effects of assessment reform has been illustrated by reports of our early findings.

Chapter 11

Thinking Skills in Higher Education: The Meno Project

John Hamilton

The last ten years or so have seen some very substantial changes in the UK educational scene. Not least has been the growth in the number of 'non-standard' entrants to higher education: entrants who do not possess the school leaving certificates which, in the not too distant past, were the necessary passport to university. So great has been the growth in non-standard entry to universities that the traditional entrants, moving from school to university around the age of 18, are now a minority of those entering degree-level courses. At the same time, post-secondary educational provision has become increasingly diverse, and the old model of progression, whereby at the end of each stage of education a minority went forward to the next, is now difficult to discern. If that model could be described as something like a distillation apparatus, the new model is more like a complex wiring diagram, with a great many possible routes through the multitude of courses on offer.

For a body like the University of Cambridge Local Examinations Syndicate, a provider of secondary school curricula and school leaving examinations, there was a clear need to develop a new approach to curriculum and assessment, one which would support the new educational pattern as it was emerging. The result is the Meno Thinking Skills Service.

The Service has been developed by a team of educators and other professionals. It has moved through various stages over the period 1987 – 94, from an early stage of psychometric aptitude test development, through an intermediate stage of developing a model of thinking skills, to the present stage of a service which is orientated towards the needs and aspirations of those aiming to become higher education students. These three stages represent a development which has focused, in turn, on assessment (and on the quality of reliability), on the curriculum (and on the search for a valid model of its implicit skills), and finally on a service which would be useful to potential students (and would therefore seek both to acknowledge past experience and to look forward to possible developmental paths). At each stage, elements of the previous stage or stages have been incorporated and developed.

The rationale may be described with reference to Figure 11.1 which relates potential students to 'assessment' and 'curriculum' and shows the four elements of the service: skills description, learning support, orientation and guidance.

The first two elements are interlinked. In the first place, Meno presents potential students with an assessment of what in general they can do or should be able to do, in terms of the demands of the higher education curriculum. This assessment is made in terms of 'thinking skills' and may be termed the *skills description element.* Second, Meno presents a 'curriculum' which is a course in thinking skills, developed from the skills description element (or assessment) and from a knowledge of the

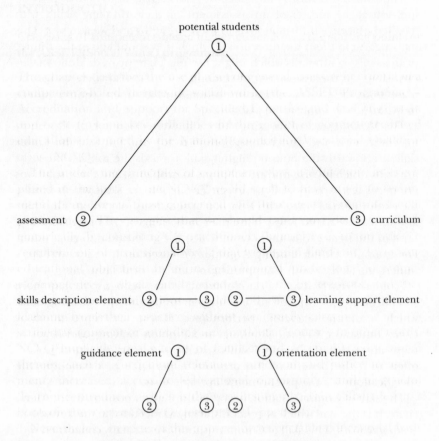

Figure 11.1 *The four elements of the Meno service*

backgrounds and experiences of potential students. This is the *learning support element*. These elements have been designed by teachers working directly for the Meno project, and also by panels of advisers drawn from nine UK institutions of higher education who worked with the Meno development team over a period of about three years. The usefulness of Meno clearly depends on the validity of their judgements.

The skills description and learning support elements provide general information and materials. The other two elements aim to provide individuals wishing to enter higher education as students with specific information useful to themselves. One of these is the *orientation element*: individuals may make use of the materials provided by the learning support element in order to assess their own potential as higher education students. The orientation element is often provided by further education colleges and within pre-degree (or 'Access') courses.

The fourth element is the *guidance element*. It is designed to provide individuals, by means of an assessment of their thinking skills, with detailed objective information as to their strengths and weaknesses. This may suggest to them the direction in which they should go in the future, or the skills or sub-skills which might usefully be improved. Meno makes provisions for the assessment of students and potential students to take place both within subscribing institutions and at 'open' centres, where individuals may apply to be assessed.

The Meno 'chart' of thinking skills is shown as Figure 11.2. The chart may be read in two dimensions: bottom to top and left to right. Lower skills are towards the bottom; higher skills towards the top. To the right are skills which involve finding solutions to problems, and these solutions are necessarily (or logically) correct. To the left are skills which involve the exploration of issues with a particular sensitivity to context. The chart also shows the sub-skills which are the components of the main skills. The lines in the figure show the ways in which the skills relate to each other. For example, Understanding Argument is based on Literacy, and is an underlying skill of both Communication and Critical Thinking.

From the early days of development, it was recognized that there should be three 'strands' to a conceptualization of the thinking skills which underpin academic performance. These are represented by Communication, Critical Thinking, and Problem Solving, and it was in these areas that the original skills specification work was undertaken, often with the benefit of the previous experience of developing the specifications for the psychometric aptitude tests.

The skill of Communication occupies the central position in the Meno chart. It is the skill which is generally acknowledged to be the key skill in academic work. This skill of Communication is essentially concerned with an understanding and use of written language. This focus upon written

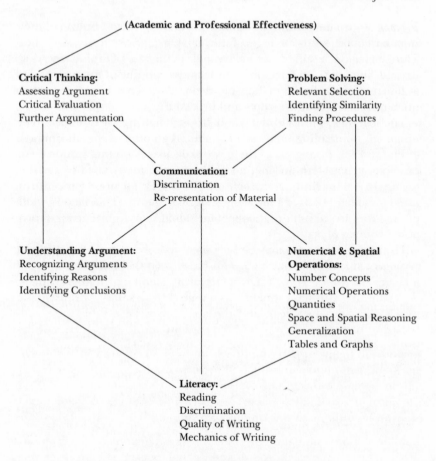

(Academic and Professional Effectiveness)

Critical Thinking:
Assessing Argument
Critical Evaluation
Further Argumentation

Problem Solving:
Relevant Selection
Identifying Similarity
Finding Procedures

Communication:
Discrimination
Re-presentation of Material

Understanding Argument:
Recognizing Arguments
Identifying Reasons
Identifying Conclusions

Numerical & Spatial Operations:
Number Concepts
Numerical Operations
Quantities
Space and Spatial Reasoning
Generalization
Tables and Graphs

Literacy:
Reading
Discrimination
Quality of Writing
Mechanics of Writing

Figure 11.2   *The Meno thinking skills*

language is not to deny the importance of spoken communication but to recognize the central place of the skills of reading and writing in higher education.

The specific abilities required within Communication have been identified by establishing what is required in the production of academic and professional writing. When writing essays or reports, students and employees need to understand information, to select from the information available that which is relevant to the subject and purpose of the essay or report, and to recombine that information in a coherent and persuasive piece of writing. These are the abilities demanded by Communication.

Based upon Communication, but also with distinctive elements of their own, are the other two academic skills of Critical Thinking and Problem

Solving. Both take ordinary language as their basis but apply to it their own particular kinds of logic: informal logic in the case of Critical Thinking, and scientific or deductive logic in the case of Problem Solving. Critical Thinking also demands a basic understanding of the structure of argument, while Problem Solving demands a knowledge of certain numerical and spatial concepts and procedures.

The skills of Critical Thinking and Problem Solving are intended to be insightful, demanding that a student should go beyond the information given (and this distinguishes these two skills from Communication). For example, in Problem Solving, insight may be demonstrated by restructuring data or by finding analogies in the search for novel procedures, and in Critical Thinking by suggesting alternative explanations while putting forward objections, possibly including moral objections, to proposed courses of action.

The three lower skills may be seen as supportive of the academic and professional skills just outlined. The most basic skill is Literacy, and it includes the ability to read newspaper articles and information leaflets, the ability to pick out information as required (for example, from a guide to television programmes), and the ability to write a short essay with regard to both the coherence of the content and the mechanics of the writing (for example, punctuation and spelling). Understanding Argument includes the ability to recognize arguments, the ability to identify the conclusions in arguments, and the ability to identify the reasons which may lead to particular conclusions being drawn. Numerical and Spatial Operations demands knowledge of six sub-skills: number concepts (for example, knowing that 100 is 10×10); numerical operations (addition, subtraction, multiplication, division); quantities (for example, litres, metres, minutes); space and spatial reasoning (for example, knowing the shape of a cube); generalization (for example, identifying patterns in sequences of numbers); and the interpretation of tables and graphs (for example, as provided in newspapers).

Academic and Professional Effectiveness provides an over-arching capacity at the top of the Meno chart, but it is not a Meno skill, and for two reasons. First, there is more to Academic and Professional Effectiveness than thinking ability. Other aspects of personality, including motivation, are crucial. Second, personal effectiveness is related to the unique demands which an academic or professional situation places on an individual. Academic and Professional Effectiveness is often appropriately supported by Records of Achievement, performance reviews, action planning, staff appraisal procedures, and the like.

It may be observed here that these general academic skills or 'thinking skills' may often be different from 'vocational skills', for example business skills or technological skills, in the sense that the former, if acknowledged at all, are usually subsumed within the knowledge and understanding of particular domains, while the latter are often primary, being applicable to a range of environments.

In judging the relevance of thinking skills to higher education curricula, there are a number of issues which would seem to focus on the relationship of the skills to content or, expressed differently, the question of whether the same skill can have both general application (which is implicit in the Meno rationale), and specific applications (as in an academic course of study). These issues may be viewed in relation to an appraisal of the guidance element which aims to replicate academic work, albeit using material which is accessible to the Meno clientele.

It is, unfortunately, rather difficult to give even a flavour of the learning support element in the limited space available here. At the present time, specially prepared materials are available in the four lower skills. These have been written by experts in the field who, in most cases, have been associated with the development of Meno from the beginning. For Critical Thinking and Problem Solving, students and potential students are referred to textbooks. In order to give some rough idea of the abilities which the learning support materials aim to develop in people, Figures 11.3 and 11.4 show respectively the kinds of questions which proficient critical thinkers and proficient problem solvers are expected to be able to attempt with confidence.

Turning to the orientation element, the key issues are whether individuals, particularly those who intend to return to formal education, are genuinely helped by the guidance provided; and whether colleges will find Meno suitable as an instrument which can orientate people towards academic work. At the time of writing, these questions are unanswered, but there is genuine enthusiasm and optimism on the part of both the Meno team and those who intend to use Meno, for example with Access students. As refinements and improvements suggest themselves, there should be no difficulty in adjusting the orientation package which, as supplied to educational institutions, includes training materials for teachers who wish to evaluate students' essays, a guide to assessment for students, and a help-line service for teachers.

The guidance element is essentially an assessment service. Results are reported as a profile, across the skills, and also across the sub-skills within each skill. These profiles provide detailed guidance to individuals. In some cases, verbal comments may also be given.

The key issue for assessment is fairness which, in the first place, means that Meno should assess people's underlying abilities in such a way that particular groups – defined by gender, race or ethnic background, age and social class – are not disadvantaged. The material used should reflect

No electoral system will ever produce the right leaders. In order to succeed in a leadership election, one must be ambitious and single-minded. But these are not good qualities in a leader. Those who have the virtues needed in a leader – humility and open-mindedness – would not become leaders in an election, because elections are necessarily competitive.

Which one of the following best expresses the main conclusion of the argument above?

(A) Ambition and single-mindedness are necessary in a leader.

(B) Humility and open-mindedness do not help candidates to win elections.

(C) People who win elections are never the right leaders.

(D) Humble and open-minded individuals are desirable as leaders.

(E) The major fault of the electoral system is its competitiveness.

The correct answer is (C)

*   *   *

This question asks you to identify the main conclusion of the argument. As explained earlier, an argument consists of **reasons** offered in support of a **conclusion**. The first thing to do is to ask yourself, 'What is the **main point** which this argument tries to get me to accept or believe?' You can underline the sentence which you think expresses the main point. Then check that the rest of the passage seems to be a good reason or a series of good reasons for accepting this main point. This should help you to see whether you have really chosen the main conclusion, or just an intermediate conclusion, which is one step in the reasoning to the main conclusion. You may know whether the reasons are true, but you don't need to worry about this. Just ask yourself, 'Suppose these reasons are true, would they give me good reason to accept the conclusion?'

This argument seems to be trying to convince us that an electoral system cannot produce the right leaders, so our first move would be to underline the first sentence of the passage. We then need to see whether the rest of the passage gives support to this claim. The rest of the passage gives two reasons which would support the claim made in the first sentence. They are:

(i)   that, in order to get elected as a leader, you need to have the wrong qualities for leadership (ie ambition and single-mindedness).

> (ii)   that having the right qualities for leadership (ie humility and open-mindedness) would prevent you from getting elected as a leader.
>
> We may not know whether these two reasons are true, but if they were, they would be good reasons for believing that the first sentence is true. So, it seems clear that the first sentence of the passage is being offered as a conclusion.

Figure 11.3   *An example of Meno assessment of critical thinking*

people's informal interests, jobs and everyday lives. Social inequalities should have less effect in Meno than in achievement tests.

To these ends, all assessment materials are reviewed by a sensitivity committee and revised or removed if necessary in order to avoid using insensitive or inappropriate content. The intention is that the content of the assessment should reflect the multicultural and social mix of those likely to be taking the assessment. Any material that is seen potentially to perpetuate stereotypes or to offend members of a particular group, or which might otherwise upset or distract students on the basis of their sex, race or ethnic origin, age or disability, is not used.

Other assessment issues include the need to use appropriate techniques for the assessment of the various skills, and the need for procedures to ensure that the standards applied are equated across different forms of the same skill assessment. The first of these needs is met by the use of both objective and essay techniques of assessment; the second by the use of statistical equating procedures (objective assessments) and by the use of general grading criteria applied with all forms of essay assessments in a particular skill.

Meno is intended to be used flexibly. Looking again at Figure 11.1, it can be seen that potential students may start with the skills description and guidance elements, or with the learning support and orientation elements. Indeed, they may use only one of these pairs of elements. Teachers may be expected to favour the 'curriculum' as a starting point, but individuals who believe they possess thinking skills and wish to gain certificates may go straight into an assessment.

A course in thinking skills does not have to start with the Meno 'curriculum'. A class of potential higher education students may have particular needs which could, for example, mean developing or using a somewhat different course, perhaps as a preliminary to the use of the Meno materials.

Similarly the Meno assessment may be viewed as either criterion-

The following figures are the numbers of scientific staff at the Italian Antarctic base in its first six years:

    12   31   82   78   122   114

If all the staff work for exactly three years in a row, what is the smallest number that there could be in the seventh year?

   (A)   114

   (B)   106

   (C)   44

   (D)   40

   (E)   36

The correct answer is (B).

Finding a solution depends upon finding a method of restructuring the information given so that it becomes apparent how many scientists arrive in each year. The table shows the number of scientists broken down into the groups in which they arrive.

YEAR	1	2	3	4	5	6	7		
	12	12	12	first year's intake					
		19	19	19	second year's intake				
			51	51	51				
				8	8	8			
					63	63	63		
						43	43	43	
							0	0	0

If no scientists join in year 7 the total is 106.

Figure 11.4 *An example of Meno assessment of problem-solving*

referenced (referenced to the curriculum) or as norm-referenced (referenced to the average performance of a group of people, for example those in a particular class). There is, however, a third mode of assessment-referencing, sometimes called ipsative or person-referenced assessment. Ipsative referencing is the interpretation of results in relation to an individual's previous result or expected result. Many people view thinking skills as abilities which develop over time and person-referencing is entirely appropriate to the sensitive use of Meno, which means that students' pieces of work and guidance profiles should be interpreted in relation to their background experiences.

Research will be crucial to the further development of Meno and to its acceptance by the educational community. The kind of research associated with the guidance element is mainly statistical. It encompasses both reliability (or consistency) and an investigation of bias effects. Reliability studies have so far been carried out on item (or question) internal consistency, and (for essay questions) marking consistency, with satisfactory results. The consistency of results for students attempting different forms of the same skill assessment has yet to be investigated.

All who attempt a Meno assessment are asked to provide, confidentially, certain personal information by means of a questionnaire, and a statistical procedure, Differential Item Functioning analysis, is used to identify questions where one group performs better than another group in spite of similar levels of skill as determined by their performance overall. Such questions are scrutinized to determine the most appropriate action. In some cases questions are deleted or they might be included in an assessment where compensatory questions counteract their effect.

The research associated with the orientation element is more judgemental, and may be termed an investigation of usefulness. How do teachers and students react to this element of Meno? Does Meno raise awareness of the kinds of thinking demanded in higher education, and does it help to make students feel positive about their own futures as students in higher education? Some answers should emerge fairly soon.

The research linked to the skills description element and to the learning support element is more fundamental. Research into the skills description element, in the first instance, takes the form of an investigation of constructs: to what extent do the Meno skills represent separate human capacities? And, to what extent are the sub-skills within each skill separately identifiable? Some preliminary results are available, but more extensive analyses are awaited. These results will almost certainly cause a reappraisal of the Meno chart, and possibly some changes in its design.

The last aspect of research is probably the most fundamental of all: does the learning support element develop *transferable* skills? The answer may well depend on the way in which this element is delivered, for it seems sensible to expect the prospect of transferability to be improved if the skills are taught as being transferable, and are demonstrated across a wide range of applications. Further development and refinement of the learning support materials will almost certainly be demanded.

Finally, why 'Meno'? Meno was a pupil of Socrates who, in the course of a discussion on the acquisition of 'virtue', prompted Socrates to propound his theory of knowledge as recollection. When Meno asked for a demonstration of the theory, Socrates proceeded to lead a young slave through a series of questions to the solution of a mathematical problem. In this experiment, Socrates claimed not to have told the slave anything, but to have elicited knowledge which the slave already possessed.

The story of Meno may be interpreted today as indicating that many people may be capable of learning much more than they realize. It is this belief which drives the Meno project, and it is a belief shared by an increasing number of educators.

This brief survey of the Meno Thinking Skills Service is inevitably a snapshot view of the project's state of development at a particular time. From 1995, the Service is being made generally available, and it is to be hoped that this will raise awareness of the role which thinking skills may play in educational theory and practice.

Chapter 12

The Impact of General National Vocational Qualifications on Higher Education

Christoph Williams

INTRODUCTION

This chapter identifies the potential influence of General National Vocational Qualifications (GNVQs) on institutions of higher education. The focus is not upon the possible impact of the development of GNVQs at higher levels but upon the impact on HE of a growing number of entrants who have followed GNVQ courses prior to admission. It outlines some characteristics of GNVQ qualifications and of the students studying them. Students' expectations and issues of continuity and progression are then discussed and a number of recommendations made for staff development in the higher education sector.

THE LIKELY UPTAKE OF GNVQS

Clearly, the impact of GNVQs on higher education will be partly determined by their uptake. Out of the predicted 46,000 advanced level candidates for 1994/5, somewhere in the region of 8–15,000 candidates are expected to apply to higher education, either directly or through the Universities and Colleges Admissions Service (UCAS). In the 1993/4 pilot year, 3,700 students embarked upon an advanced level GNVQ, of whom approximately one-quarter (905) applied to higher education via UCAS (UCAS, personal communication, 1994).

The higher education sector has been broadly categorized as being composed of the pastoral/tutorial Oxbridge institutions with the new universities of the 1960s and the vocational/community-based civic universities and polytechnics (NIACE, 1993). Due to their vocational emphasis, organizations in the latter category tend to be more attractive to GNVQ candidates. The *percentage* of offers made by both types of institutions to these individuals do not (to date) differ significantly (*ibid*). Hence, the larger number of GNVQ candidates progressing onto the latter category of institutions appears to be due to a greater *number* of applications being made as opposed to different rates of acceptance. In other words, students from a GNVQ background are applying in greater numbers to the 'new' universities.

In addition to national trends, there may be localized variations caused by formal local initiatives such as the COMPACT schemes or less formal partnerships. Arguably, an over-reliance on such arrangements could reduce the success rate of cross-regional applications from GNVQ students. However, considering the projected number of GNVQ applications to higher education (see Table 12.1), this scenario of an over-application to the higher education sector is unlikely to materialize. The figures shown in the table are approximate, exclude the intermediate GNVQ and assume a continuation of the current rate of entry to higher education or employment.

The spread of modularization and the development of a national credit accumulation and transfer scheme (and the associated credit framework) are likely to be of relevance, as is the proposed development of a two-year Associate Degree with potential dual GNVQ level 4 accreditation. A recent report on credit accumulation and transfer states that,

> To meet the specification of an Associate Degree as an academic qualification, but not as a GNVQ4, the student programme should contain no less than 25% of credit for core skills. To meet the specifications of an Associate Degree as an academic qualification and as GNVQ4, the student programme should contain no less than 40% but no more than 50% of credit for core skills (Robertson, 1994, p. 158).

Table 12.1 *Projected applications to higher education by GNVQ candidates (source: UCAS, personal communication)*

Year	Total number of GNVQ candidates	Number of GNVQ candidates applying to higher education
1994	3,700	905
1995	46,452	15,000
1996	70,000	23,000
1997	200,000	66,000

These developments will require higher education institutions to provide programmes of study that are flexible enough to provide differential emphases upon the core skills units.

It is also worth noting that the current trends in A level provision are bringing them closer to GNVQs, with a growing interest in modularity, more continuous assessment, the broader reporting of candidates' achievements, subject cores and the articulation of assessment objectives that are explicitly linked to the grades awarded. Further, as the awareness and understanding of GNVQs increases, a greater level of overall acceptance might be expected. Finally, there is always the possibility that the higher education sector could be pressurized to accept GNVQs. Pressure could come from government funding policies or via the careers services of further education institutions which could boycott specific universities.

In sum, a growing number of applicants to universities will have GNVQs and A levels are taking on some characteristics of GNVQs. These developments have the potential to make universities change some aspects of their provision.

SOME CHARACTERISTICS OF GNVQS AND THEIR IMPACT ON STUDENTS

First, GNVQ assessment involves the collection of evidence against the specified requirements of each unit of learning. Learning outcomes (describing what students should know or be able to do upon the completion of each unit) ensure students have a clear understanding of what they are expected to achieve. The type of evidence they need in order to demonstrate this achievement is specified by the use of evidence indicators. The students are also aware that their performance will be assessed against general criteria concerning their ability to plan, to seek and handle information and to evaluate. Thus GNVQs are an assessment framework with clearly defined assessment criteria, providing students and institutions with some autonomy over the learning process through which they work towards mastery of these criteria.

Second, GNVQs involve a wide variety of classroom-based assignments, including:

- project work
- coursework/progression assignments
- internal tests
- reports of work-based elements of the course

- essays

- short-answer questions, case studies and multiple-choice tests for each mandatory unit (70 per cent required to pass).

These are incorporated into a portfolio of evidence (or National Record of Achievement) providing a profile of personal skills, an individual action plan (requiring student involvement in their destiny) and a record of personal development. Non-academic work may also be included (eg, testimonials and references derived from workplace-based experience).

Third, GNVQs should involve:

- active learning (directed by the national standards)

- regular feedback on performance

- individual reflection and planning

- negotiation of and participation in both the assessment process and the learning contract.

The learning process on GNVQ programmes is very active, with assessment based primarily on the portfolio of evidence. The recording and assessment of achievement, action planning and negotiation, etc., mean that students are accustomed to regular feedback on their performance and progress. Further, personal reflection (upon previous learning) is required for students to negotiate where evidence can be used for assessment purposes and to influence the shape of their future learning.

Fourth, GNVQs are flexible and enhance learner autonomy. The inherent flexibility of GNVQs, notably in the form of the optional and additional units, provides students with greater control over what they learn, although practical considerations mean that the range of modules provided may be more restricted. It also provides a qualification with a potentially different 'flavour' ie, flexibility can lead to extra specialization, providing a deeper understanding of the areas covered or an extended menu of subjects implying a greater breadth of understanding.

The balance between theory and practical work reflects the view that GNVQs provide a route to either higher education or employment. As students may not know their preferred destination at the start of their programme of study, it is appropriate that it can evolve with time.

Flexibility in the core skills units allows individuals with particular talents, for example numeracy, or interests, for example information technology, to progress onto higher GNVQ levels. Hence, individuals with particular abilities in the core skills areas should be used to continued progression and advancement. Arguably, the emphasis placed on personal transferable skills may result in GNVQ students being more advanced in these areas than 'traditional' students.

Some have suggested that GNVQ students tend to be well-motivated and self-reliant. This could be because the GNVQ learning experience provides them with empowerment, that is with greater ownership of and responsibility for their own learning, since they should be used to influencing the direction of their learning and the learning processes through which required evidence of achievement is generated. Alternatively, GNVQ students may be self-selecting, which is to say that individuals with these characteristics may be more likely to select the GNVQ path as part of their academic career.

GNVQ students may also develop (or possess) a different learning style relative to traditional students. Individuals' responsibility for relating what is learnt to their previous experience, for playing with ideas and exploring potential connections and discrepancies, is likely to result in the development of an active, explorative learning style. This could be contrasted with what has often been seen as a pervasive, more passive, reproductive, mechanical learning style associated with the recall of facts and information resulting in a more superficial understanding.

CONTINUITY AND PROGRESSION: IMPLICATIONS FOR HIGHER EDUCATION

There is, then, a strong case for believing that there will be more higher education students coming from a GNVQ or, indeed, an NVQ background. They are more likely to be independent learners and to have different needs and expectations compared to the traditional university entrant. The ethos and culture of GNVQs means that these students are likely to expect more individualized programmes of study, the use of active learning methods and assessment based upon clearly specified criteria/learning outcomes and correspondingly detailed feedback.

Induction programmes need to allow these individuals to unpack their achievements and express their aspirations. Students may expect a portfolio and profiling approach to learner-support and guidance, to recording achievements and to the identification of individual learning paths even – or especially – within modularized schemes. Many institutions offering GNVQs or A levels have invested heavily in tutorial systems. Thus the often weak tutorial systems and the apparent low incidence of student-centred learning approaches characteristic of higher education may be equally alien to applicants with a GNVQ background and, increasingly, to those with A levels.

So, additional support may be required for successful adaptation to the current culture of higher education and it is possible that more assistance will be needed to help learners to develop essay writing and examination skills. Admittedly, there is the possibility that some students will be familiar with these techniques as there are no restrictions in GNVQs on the use of these forms of assessment. Moreover, some students may have difficulty with the pace of higher education, as there are no time limits on the completion of a GNVQ.

At the same time, many universities are reappraising their missions and goals and recognize that the emphasis placed by GNVQs upon transferable skills such as communication ought to be continued in higher education. Equally, specific skills that can be of use in the workplace, such as data analysis, are increasingly seen as worthy objects of universities' attention. It is becoming accepted that opportunities are needed for students to demonstrate that they can transfer these skills to different contexts. Some institutions, of which the Open University is one, are considering the incorporation of higher-level core skill units into their degree-level courses, while supplementary core skills units covering personal skills, problem-solving and modern foreign languages, amongst others, are already available.

If GNVQ students are orientated towards an active, participative style of learning, then they are less likely to respond well to highly structured forms of teaching and assessments such as traditional lectures and examinations. Universities trying to accommodate themselves to such students will consider many developments; for example, more interactive and thought-provoking teaching styles that will encourage student involvement, creativity and the ability to deal and cope with change; detailed and prompt feedback; hands-on, practical work-related case studies and projects, research projects and placements; realistic simulations; open-ended assessments, oral assessments, self- and peer-assessment; formative assessments; and student-delivered lectures and seminars.

The use of more explicit assessment criteria, which might be expressed in terms of learning outcomes, may be used to guide both teaching and learning. The acquisition of credits for the completion of a module will be a relatively novel experience to those new students coming from a GNVQ background, as in theory only core skills units are graded independently in a GNVQ qualification. Care will be needed to ensure modules do not differ greatly in their workload and assessment demands, which will only compound GNVQ entrants' difficulties with common higher education practices. Yet, while the use of learning outcomes in higher education is becoming more conventional, it is still problematic. For example, too many learning outcomes for a module may not only confuse and scare students but also prevent them from independently exploring other areas, whether directly related to the module or not.

Care is required to ensure similar learning outcomes are not covered and assessed in different modules, leading to a situation that was once familiar in schools, where some aims were over-taught while others were virtually neglected. Tackling this could prove difficult under a modularized system where it may be difficult to predict which modules students will select. Furthermore, some learning outcomes may be more easily addressed in a variety of module settings than others can be. It is worth noting that a more standardized approach to the identification and definition of learning outcomes in modules, units and programmes has contentious implications for academic freedom.

Additional complications may arise due to different interpretations of what learning outcomes actually mean or represent (see, for example, Chapters 4 and 5, this volume). These differences may occur both between and within student/staff groups. Further, can criteria be developed that distinguish between the different levels of study, or, indeed, different degree classifications that are practically useful and meaningful to students and staff alike? Students are likely to expect a clear link between the assessment methods employed and the learning outcomes covered. Again, too many learning outcomes might lead to an over-emphasis on assessment as students struggle to meet each of the specified criteria encompassed by any one module. There is also the recurrent danger in modularization that students may perceive a degree programme as being composed of discrete modular blocks rather than as being a coherent, integrated whole.

Finally, can – and should – everything that might be included under the banner of the added-value obtained from an experience in higher education be neatly defined, categorized and assessed? To be specific, should higher education institutions be assessing the development of cultural and social values and of personal qualities?

Considering the pace of the introduction of GNVQs and NVQs, there is clearly an urgent need for staff development to:

- Extend academics' knowledge and understanding of the different programmes that students will have followed prior to entry and to promote an awareness of the greater diversity of learning styles that they will have experienced.

- Raise awareness of the need for the provision of appropriate academic support and guidance for students, for example through the process of generating portfolios of evidence, by ensuring student understanding of learning objectives and assessment criteria, and through the negotiation of learning contracts.

- Assist in the generation of appropriate learning outcomes and in making explicit the linkages these should have with assessment methods.

- Foster greater flexibility in assessment methods and teaching styles.

- Inform colleagues about the NVQ certification process, including the quality assurance system of training and assessor awards.

- Develop appropriate mechanisms for the Accreditation of Prior (Experiential) Learning.

CONCLUSION

It remains to be seen how higher level GNVQs will directly affect higher education. What is certain is that an increasing number of applicants to universities will have followed GNVQ programmes and have different expectations and needs than 'traditional' applicants have had. Responding to these expectations and needs should involve higher education in substantial changes to the ways in which learners are assessed and taught. The argument is not simply that these changes are something that GNVQ students are entitled to expect but also that they are changes that are inherently valuable.

References

Argyris, C and Schön, DA (1974) *Theory into Practice: Increasing professional effectiveness,* San Francisco, CA: Jossey-Bass.

Ashworth, P and Saxton, J (1990) 'On competence', *Journal of Further and Higher Education,* **14**, 2, 3–25.

Assiter, A and Shaw, E (eds) (1993) *Using Records of Achievement in Higher Education,* London: Kogan Page.

Atkins, MJ, Beattie, J and Dockrell, WB (1993) *Assessment Issues in Higher Education,* Sheffield: Employment Department.

Baric, L (1993) 'The settings approach: implications for policy and strategy', *Journal of the Institute of Health Education,* **30**, 1, 17–24.

Barnes, D (1989) *Active Learning,* Leeds: University of Leeds, TVEI Support Unit.

Barnett, R (1992) *Improving Higher Education,* Buckingham: Open University Press/SRHE.

Barnett, R (1994) *The Limits of Competence,* Buckingham: Open University Press/ SRHE.

Beattie, A (1990) *Teaching and Learning about Health Education: New directions in curriculum development,* Edinburgh: Health Education Board for Scotland.

Beattie, A (1991) 'Knowledge and control in health promotion: a test-case for social theory and social policy', in Gabe, J, Calnan, M and Bury, M (eds) *Sociology of the Health Service,* London: Routledge.

Bereiter, C and Scardamalia, M (1993) *Surpassing Ourselves: An inquiry into the nature and implications of expertise,* Chicago and La Salle, Ill: Open Court.

Black, H, (1992), *Standards in Museums: A study of the means of conveying the meaning of NVQ/SVQ standards in the museums sector,* Edinburgh: The Scottish Council for Research in Education.

Black, H, Hall, J, Martin, S and Yates, J (1989) *The Quality of Assessments: Case-studies in the National Certificate,* Edinburgh: The Scottish Council for Research in Education.

Bloom, BS (1956) *Taxonomy of Educational Objectives, Volume 1, The cognitive domain,* Harlow: Longman.

Boyatzis, R (1982) *The Competent Manager: A model for effective performance,* New York: John Wiley.

Broadfoot, P (ed.) (1980) *Profiles and Records of Achievement: A review of issues and practice,* London: Cassell.

Broadfoot, P (1990) *The Way Forward for RoA,* London: University of London.

Brown, S and Knight, P (1994) *Assessing Learners in Higher Education*, London: Kogan Page.

BTEC (1992) *Implementing BTEC GNVQs; An interim guide, issue no. 1*, London: BTEC.

Bunton, R and MacDonald, G (1992) *Health Promotion: Disciplines and diversity*, London: Routledge.

Burgoyne, J and Stuart, R (1976) 'The nature, use and acquisition of managerial skills and other attributes', *Personnel Review*, **5**, 4, 19–29.

Caplan, R (1993) 'The importance of social theory for health promotion', *Health Promotion International*, **8**, 2, 147–57.

Caplan, R and Holland, R (1990) 'Rethinking health education theory', *Health Education Journal*, **49**, 1, 10–12.

Carter, RG (1985) 'A taxonomy of objectives for professional education', *Studies in Higher Education*, **10**, 2, 135–49.

Carter, RG and Cooke, F (1987) 'An accelerated experience course in project engineering', *Electronics and Power*, **33**, 101–4.

Challis, M, Usherwood, T and Joesbury, H (1993) *Assessing Specified Competences in Medical Training, Technical Report number 16*, Sheffield: Employment Department, Methods Strategy Unit.

Challis, M, Usherwood, T and Joesbury, H (1994) *Assessment of Specified Competences in Undergraduate General Practice Medical Training, Technical Report number 21*, Sheffield: Employment Department, Methods Strategy Unit.

Coventry University (1994) *Guide to the Enterprise Code of Practice*, Coventry: Coventry University.

Department for Education (1992) *Circular 9/92: Initial Teacher Training (Secondary Phase)*, London: DfE.

Department for Education (1993a) *Circular 14/93: The Initial Training of Primary School Teachers, New criteria for courses*, London: DfE.

Department for Education (1993b) *The Government's Proposals for the Reform of Initial Teacher Training*, London: DfE.

Department of Education and Science (1992) *HMI Report: A Survey of the Enterprise Initiative in Higher Education Initiative in Fifteen Polytechnics and Colleges of Higher Education*, London: DES.

Department of Education, Northern Ireland (1993) *Review of Initial Teacher Training in Northern Ireland: Report of the working group on competences*, DENI: Belfast.

Department of Trade and Industry (1994) *Competitiveness: Helping business to win*, London: DTI.

Didsbury School of Education (1993) *Policy for the Professional Preparation of Teachers*, Manchester: The Manchester Metropolitan University, internal paper.

Didsbury School of Education (1994) *Seeds of a Way Forward: Towards a possible structure of competences*, Manchester: The Manchester Metropolitan University, internal paper.

Dixon, NF (1988) *Preconscious Processing*, Chichester, Wiley.

Downie, RS, Fyfe, C and Tannahill, A (1990) *Health Promotion Models and Values*, Oxford, Oxford Medical.

Draper, P, Griffiths, J, Dennis, J and Popay, J (1979) 'Three types of health education', *British Medical Journal*, 16 August, 495–8.

Dreyfus, HL and Dreyfus, SE (1986) *Mind over Machine: The power of human intuition and expertise in the era of the computer*, New York: Macmillan.

Edwards, A (1994) 'The impact of ITT partnerships on schools: alternative narratives', paper presented to the British Educational Research Association Annual Conference.

Edwards, A and Brunton, D (1993) 'Supporting reflection in teachers' learning', in Calderhead, J and Gates, P (eds) *Conceptualising Reflection in Teacher Development*, London: Falmer Press.

Edwards, A and Collison, J (in press) 'Partnerships in school-based teacher training – a new vision', in McBride, R (ed.) *Teacher Education Policy: Some issues arising from research and practice*, London: Falmer Press.

Elliott, J (1991) 'Competence based training and the education of the professions: is a happy marriage possible?', in Elliott, J (ed.) *Action Research for Educational Change*, Buckingham: Open University Press.

Elliott, J (1994) 'Self-evaluation and teacher competence', paper presented at Conference of Educational Studies Association of Northern Ireland, Limerick.

Employment Department (1994) *Enterprise in Higher Education – The First Eleven*, Sheffield: Employment Department.

Entwistle, N (1992) *The Impact of Learning Outcomes in Higher Education*, Sheffield: Universities Staff Development Unit/Employment Department.

Eraut, M (1994) *Developing Professional Knowledge and Competence*, London: Falmer Press.

Eraut, M and Cole, G (1993) *Assessing Competence in the Professions, Technical Report number 14*, Sheffield: Employment Department, Methods Strategy Unit.

Evans, V and Lee, J (1990) *Health Promoting Schools: A training manual*, Salford: TACADE.

Fenwick, A, Assiter, A and Nixon, N (1992) *Profiling in Higher Education – Guidelines for the development and use of profiling schemes*, London: CNAA.

Field, J (1991) 'Competency and the pedagogy of labour', *Studies in the Education of Adults*, **23**,1, 41–52.

Fish, D, Twinn, S and Purr, B (1990) *How to Enable Learning through Professional Practice*, London: West London Institute of Higher Education.

Fish, S (1994) *There is no Such Thing as Free Speech ... and it's a good thing too*, Oxford: Oxford University Press.

Fleming, D (1991) 'The concept of meta competence', *Competence and Assessment*, **16**, 1–4.

Furlong, J (1992) 'The limits of competence: a cautionary note on circular 9/92', paper presented at UCET Conference, Oxford.

Gagné, RM (1965) *Conditions of Learning*, 1st edn, New York: Holt, Rinehart and Winston.

Gellatly, A (ed.) (1986) *The Skilful Mind: An introduction to cognitive psychology*, Buckingham: Open University Press.

Gonczi, A (1994) 'Competency based assessment in the professions in Australia', *Assessment in Education*, **1**, 1, 27–44.

Greenwood, B and Hustler, D (1994) *The Recording Achievement and Higher Education Project*, Cheltenham: Universities Central Admissions Service/Employment Department.

Greenwood, B and Ward, R (1993) *The Recording Achievement and Higher Education Project 1991–93: A collection of case studies*, Cheltenham: Universities Central Admissions Service.

Hager, P (1994) 'Is there a cogent philosophical argument against competency standards?', *Australian Journal of Education*, **38**, 1, 3–18.

Harvey, L (1994) *Employer Satisfaction Survey*, Birmingham: Quality in Higher Education, University of Central England.

Health Education Authority (1993) *Health Promoting Hospitals: Principles and practice*, London: HEA.

Hyland, T (1993) 'Professional development and competence-based education', *Educational Studies*, **19**, 1, 123–32.

Issitt, M (1994) 'Competency-based approach: advantages and disadvantages', paper presented at Workshop, Postgraduate Health Education Lecturers' Forum, Winchester.

Issitt, M and Woodward, M (1992) 'Competence and contradiction', in Carter, P, Jeffs, T and Smith, MK (eds) *Changing Social Work and Welfare*, Buckingham: Open University Press.

Jessup, G (1991) *Outcomes: NVQs and the emerging model of education and training*, London: Falmer Press.

Jones, L (1992) 'Health at work', in Beattie, A, Jones, L and Sidall, M (eds) *Debates and Decisions in Everyday Health*, Milton Keynes: Open University.

Jones, L and Moore, R (1993) 'Education, competence and the control of expertise', *British Journal of the Sociology of Education*, **14**, 4, 385–97.

Kelchtermans, G (1993) 'Teachers and their career story: A biographical perspective on professional development', in Day, C, Calderhead, J and Denicolo, P (eds) *Research on Teacher Thinking: Understanding professional development.* London: Falmer Press.

Kelly, G (1955) *The Psychology of Personal Constructs*, New York: Norton.

Kelly, MP, Charlton, BG and Hanlon, P (1993) 'The four levels of health promotion: an integrated approach', *Public Health*, **107**, 319–26.

Klemp, GO (1977) 'Three factors of success – relating work and education', in Vermilye, DW (ed.) *Current Issues in Higher Education*, San Francisco, CA: Jossey-Bass.

Knight, P (1991) '"Value added" and history in public sector higher education', *PUSH Newsletter*, 3(1), 23–31.

Knight, P (ed.) (1994) *University-wide Change, Staff and Curriculum Development*, Birmingham: Staff and Educational Development Association.

Knight, P (ed.) (1995a) *Assessment for Learning in Higher Education*, London: Kogan Page.

Knight, P (1995b) *Records of Achievement in Higher and Further Education*, Lancaster: The Framework Press.

Koberg, D and Bagnall, J, (1981) *The Universal Traveller*, Los Altos, CA: William Kaufman Inc.

Kolb, DA and Fry, R (1976) 'Towards an applied theory of experiential learning', in Cooper, CL (ed.) *Theories of Group Processes*, Chichester: Wiley.

Lessem, R (1984) 'The gestalt of action learning', in Cox, C and Beck, J (eds) *Management Development – Advances in practice and theory*, Chichester: Wiley.

Levy, M (1987) *The Core Skills Project and Work-based Learning*, Coombe Lodge: Further Education Staff College.

Manpower Services Commission and Department of Education and Science (1986) *Review of Vocational Qualifications in England and Wales: Report by the working group*, London: HMSO.

Mansfield, PA (1986) 'Patchwork pedagogies: a case study of supervisors' emphasis on pedagogy in post-lesson conference', *Journal of Education for Teaching*, **12**, 3, 259–71.

Mitchell, L and Bartram, D (1994) *The Place of Knowledge and Understanding in the Development of National Vocational Qualifications and Scottish Vocational Qualifications*, Sheffield: Employment Department.

Morgan, G (1986) *Images of Organisation*, London: Sage.

Murphy, R *et al.* (1993) 'Profiling in initial teacher training', *Journal of Teacher Development*, **2**, 3, 141–6.

National Council for Vocational Qualifications (1991) *Guide to National Vocational Qualifications*, London: NCVQ. (This will be superseded in 1995 by a new edition.)

National Foundation for Educational Research (1991) *Enterprise in Higher Education, Second Year National Evaluation*, Windsor: NFER.

National Health Service Executive (1994) *Health Promoting Hospitals*, Leeds: Department of Health.

NIACE (1993) *An Adult Education: A vision*, Leicester: NIACE.

Norris, N (1991) 'The trouble with competence', *Cambridge Journal of Education*, **21**, 3, 331–41.

Novak, J and Gowin, R (1984) *Learning How to Learn*, New York: Cambridge University Press.

Oates, T (1994) 'Taking care to look where you are going: caution and credit framework developments', in Young, MFD *et al.* (eds) *Building a Credit Framework – Opportunities and problems*, London: Post-16 Education Centre, University of London Institute of Education.

O'Donnell, T and Gray, G (1993) *The Health Promoting College*, London: HEA.

Otter, S (1992) *Learning Outcomes in Higher Education*, London: UDACE/HMSO.

Otter, S and Hadfield M (1992) *Personal Competences in Higher Education. A field trial report to the Employment Department*, Sheffield: Employment Department.

Pearce, B (1982) *The Challenge of Profiling*, Leeds: CCDU.

Pearce, B (1983) *The Need for Profiling Systems in Schools*, Leeds: CCDU.

Philo, J, Russell, J and Pettersson, G (1993) *Health at Work: A needs assessment in SWTRHA*, London: South-West Thames Regional Health Authority.

Rawson, D (1993) 'The growth of health promotion theory and its rational reconstruction: lessons from the philosophy of science', in Bunton, R and MacDonald, G (eds) *Health Promotion: Disciplines and diversity*, London: Routledge.

Reason, J (1990) *Human Error*, Cambridge: Cambridge University Press.

Robertson, D (1994) *Choosing to Change: Extending access, choice and mobility in higher education*, London: Higher Education Quality Council.

Rolls, E (1994) 'The HEA competences project', paper presented at Postgraduate Health Education Lecturers' Forum, Winchester.

Rose, N (1990) 'Psychology as a "social" science', in Parker, I and Shotter, J (eds) *Deconstructing Social Psychology*, London: Routledge.

Runciman, P (1990) 'Competence-based education and the assessment and accreditation of work-based learning', National Board for Scotland Research Report.

Ryle, G (1963) *The Concept of Mind*, Harmondsworth: Peregrine Books.

Saunders, S, Pettinger, K and Tomlinson, PD (1995) 'Prospective mentors' views on partnership in secondary teacher training', *British Educational Research Journal*, **21**, 2.

Scottish Health Education Group (1990) *Promoting Good Health: Proposals for action in schools*, Edinburgh: SHEG.

Segal, Quince and Wicksteed (Economic and Management Consultants) (1994) *Thematic Evaluation of the Enterprise in Higher Education Initiative – Report to the Employment Department*, London: Segal, Quince and Wicksteed (Economic and Management Consultants).

Smithers, A (1993) *All Our Futures*, London: Channel Four Television.

Tarsh, J (1990) 'Graduate employment and degree class', *Employment Gazette*, 496–500.

Tomlinson, PD (1992) 'Psychology and education: What went wrong – or did it?', *The Psychologist: Bulletin of the British Psychological Society*, **5**, 105–109.

Tomlinson, PD (1981) *Understanding Teaching: Interactive educational psychology*, London: McGraw Hill.

Tomlinson, PD (1995a, forthcoming) 'Can competence profiling work for effective teacher education? I. General issues', *Oxford Review of Education*, **21**, 2.

Tomlinson, PD (1995b, forthcoming) 'Can competence profiling work for effective teacher education? II. Pitfalls and principles', *Oxford Review of Education*, **21**, 3.

Tomlinson, PD (1995c) *Understanding Mentoring: Reflective strategies for school-based teacher preparation*, Buckingham: Open University Press.

Tomlinson, PD and Swift, DJ (1992) 'Teacher-educator thinking in the context of radio-assisted practice: more patchwork pedagogy?', *Teaching and Teacher Education*, **8**, 2, 159–70.

Tones, K and Tilford, S (1994) *Health Education: Effectiveness, efficiency and equity*, London: Chapman and Hall.

Training and Development Lead Body (1991) *National Standards for Training and Development*, Sheffield: Employment Department.

Tuckman, BW (1965) 'Developmental sequence in small groups', *Psychological Bulletin*, **63**, 6, 384–99.

Tuxworth, E (1989) 'Competence based education and training: background and origins', in Burke, J (ed.) *Competency Based Education and Training*, London: Falmer Press.

Twining, W (1990) *Rethinking Evidence*, Oxford: Blackwell.

Twinn, SF (1991) 'Conflicting paradigms of health visiting: a continuing debate for professional practice', *Journal of Advanced Nursing*, **16**, 966–73.

Whitty, G (1991) *Next in Line for Treatment?*, London: Goldsmiths College.

Whitty, G and Wilmott, E (1991) 'Competence-based teacher education: approaches and issues', *Cambridge Journal of Education*, **21**, 3, 309–18.

Wilson, P (1993) *Beyond 'A Basis For Credit?'*, London: Further Education Unit.

Winter, R (1989) 'Teacher appraisal and the development of professional knowledge', in Carr, W (ed.) *Quality in Teaching*, London: Falmer Press.

Winter, R (1991) *The ASSET Programme Volume II. The development and assessment of professional competences*, Chelmsford: Anglia Polytechnic.

Winter, R (1992) ' "Quality Management" or "The Educative Workplace"': alternative versions of competence-based education', *Journal of Further and Higher Education*, **16**, 3, 100–115.

Winter, R (1993a) 'The problem with educational levels (Part 1)', *Journal of Further and Higher Education*, **17**, 3, 68–84.

Winter, R (1993b) *Professional Competences at Degree Level. The ASSET programme report*, Chelmsford: Anglia Polytechnic University.

Winter, R (1994a) 'The problem with educational levels (Part 2)', *Journal of Further and Higher Education*, **18**, 1, 92–106.

Winter, R (1994b) 'The second dimension of assessment; transferable skills as general criteria for a competence-based vocational curriculum (The ASSET Model)', in Bridges, D (ed.) *Transferable Skills in Higher Education*, Norwich: University of East Anglia.

Winter, R and Maisch, M (1991) *Professionalism and Competence: The ASSET programme, volume I*, Chelmsford: Anglia Polytechnic/Essex Social Services.

Wittgenstein, L (1963) *Philosophical Investigations*, Oxford: Blackwell.

Wolf, A (1994) *Competence-based Assessment*, Buckingham: Open University Press.

Young, I and Williams, T (1990) *The Healthy School*, Edinburgh: Scottish Health Education Group.

Zeichner, K and Tabachnik, BR (1982) 'The belief systems of university supervisors in an elementary student-teaching program', *Journal of Education for Teaching*, **8**, 34–54.

Index